The
Princeton
Theology

Reformed Theology in America
Edited by David F. Wells

The Princeton Theology

Edited by
David F. Wells

 **BAKER BOOK HOUSE**
Grand Rapids, Michigan 49516

BX
9424.5
.U6
P73
1989

The material in this volume originally comprised part of a book titled *Reformed Theology in America: A History of Its Modern Development*, copyright 1985 by Wm. B. Eerdmans Publishing Company.

Printed in the United States of America

Library of Congress Cataloging-in-Publication Data

The Princeton theology / edited by David F. Wells.
    p. cm.
    "The material in this volume originally comprised part of a book titled Reformed theology in America: a history of its modern development, copyright 1985 by Wm. B. Eerdmans Publishing Company"—T.p. verso.
    Other portions of this original work republished under Southern Reformed theology and Dutch Reformed theology.
    Bibliography: p.
    Includes index.
    Contents: The Princeton theology / Mark A. Noll—Charles Hodge / David F. Wells—Benjamin B. Warfield / W. Andrew Hoffecker—J. Gresham Machen / W. Stanford Reid.
    ISBN 0-8010-9702-9
    1. Princeton theology. 2. Reformed Church—United States—Doctrines—History. 3. Presbyterian Church—United States—Doctrines—History. 4. Calvinism—United States—History. 5. Theology, Doctrinal—United States—History. 6. Theologians—United States—History. I. Wells, David F. II. Reformed theology in America.
BX9424.5.U6P73   1989
230'.57'09—dc20
                                                  89-6913
                                                   CIP

To Roger Nicole
A Man of God

CONTENTS

CONTRIBUTORS

W. Andrew Hoffecker, professor of religion at Grove City College has penned *Piety and the Princeton Theologians* (Phillipsburg, NJ: Presbyterian and Reformed, 1981) and coedited (with Gary Scott Smith) *Building a Christian World View*, 2 vols. (Phillipsburg, NJ: Presbyterian and Reformed, 1986–1988).

George M. Marsden, professor of the history of Christianity in America at The Divinity School, Duke University, is the author of *Reforming Fundamentalism: Fuller Seminary and the New Evangelicalism* (Grand Rapids: Eerdmans, 1987), *Fundamentalism and American Culture* (New York: Oxford University Press, 1980), and *The Evangelical Mind and the New School Presbyterian Experience* (New Haven: Yale University Press, 1970); coauthor (with Mark Noll and Nathan Hatch) of *The Search for Christian America* (Westchester, IL: Crossway, 1983); and editor of *Evangelicalism and Modern America* (Grand Rapids: Eerdmans, 1984).

Mark A. Noll, professor of history at Wheaton College, has coauthored (with George Marsden and Nathan Hatch) *The Search for Christian America* (Westchester, IL: Crossway, 1983), and has edited *The Princeton Theology, 1812–1921: Scripture, Science, and Theological Method from Alexander to Warfield* (Grand Rapids: Baker, 1983), *The Bible in America* (New York: Oxford University Press, 1982), and *Eerdmans' Handbook to Christianity in America* (Grand Rapids: Eerdmans, 1983).

W. Stanford Reid is professor emeritus of history, University of Guelph (Guelph, Ontario), formerly lecturer and professor of history at McGill University (Montreal, Quebec, 1941–1965), and founder and chairperson of the Department of History, University of Guelph, 1965–1970. He is the author of *The Church of Scotland in Lower Canada: Its Struggle for*

Establishment (Toronto: Thorn, 1936), *Skipper from Leith: The Life of Robert Barton of Over Barnton* (Philadelphia: University of Pennsylvania Press, 1964), *Christianity and Scholarship* (Nutley, NJ: Presbyterian and Reformed, 1966), and *Trumpeter of God: A Biography of John Knox* (New York: Charles Scribner's Sons, 1974; Grand Rapids: Baker, 1980).

David F. Wells, Andrew Mutch Professor of Historical and Systematic Theology at Gordon-Conwell Theological Seminary, has authored *Revolution in Rome* (London: Tyndale, 1973), *The Search for Salvation* (Downers Grove, IL: InterVarsity, 1978), *The Prophetic Theology of George Tyrrell* (Chico, CA: Scholars Press, 1981), *The Person of Christ: A Biblical and Historical Analysis of the Incarnation* (Westchester, IL: Crossway, 1984), *God the Evangelist: How the Holy Spirit Works to Bring Men and Women to Faith* (Grand Rapids: Eerdmans, 1987), and *Turning to God: Biblical Conversion in the Modern World* (Grand Rapids: Baker, 1989).

PREFACE

ONE of the quirks of American theology is that it is frequently unaware of being American. German theology, of course, is the result of the ponderous and enormously thorough German academic machinery from which it has emerged. British theology, with its keen interest in historical accuracy, fair play, and civility, obviously reflects the virtues of the middle and upper-middle classes in which it is largely nurtured. South American theology makes no bones about being South American. It wears its heart on its sleeve. North of the border, however, this is not so. Here, we simply do theology!

If that were really true, then we should expect to find in the various expressions of Reformed theology a striking conformity, for they are all disciplined by the Reformation principles of *sola Scriptura, sola gratia, in solo Christo,* and *sola fide.* What we actually encounter is a most astonishing variety of expression, despite the common ownership of these principles. Immigrants who have come to these shores, nurturing within themselves the Reformed faith on which they were reared, did not melt into the national pot as they were supposed to. Ethnic interests, in fact, were often preserved through language and custom even as a diffuse sense of what it meant to be American also grew in importance. And, along the way, Reformed theologies have struck up alliances with the habits of mind that have prevailed in this or that age as well as being shaped by the towering figures who, from time to time, have arisen above the tradition and given it new cogency, new direction, and sometimes new horizons. American Reformed theology, as a result, is a complex tradition made up of strands and tributaries that are not only diverse but also sometimes quite oblivious to one another.

In 1985 *Reformed Theology in America: A History of Its Modern Development* appeared. To those with eyes to see, it was a thinly disguised *Festschrift* for Roger Nicole, who was celebrating his seventieth birthday that year. But it was also a serious accounting of the Reformed tradition in all of its diversity. I chose what I saw to be the five major streams of Reformed thought: the Princeton theology, the Westminster school, the Dutch schools, the Southern tradition, and neoorthodoxy. Within each of these sections I followed the same pattern of providing readers with a general essay on the school and essays on its two most prominent theologians.

The success that attended the publication of this study was nowhere better attested than in the dozens of letters I received, as well as in the reviews which were published, that complained about this or that group which had been excluded from consideration! All of a sudden I was beset with the knowledge of numerous groups, streams, traditions, and movements that would have liked to have been recognized and felt a little aggrieved that I had not seen fit to include them! It was then that I knew that I had to seek a new publisher for this work once the Eerdmans edition had run its course.

I am deeply grateful for the willingness of Baker Book House to do this. They decided to divide the original study into three smaller books, representing the sections originally published as the Princeton theology, the Dutch schools, and the Southern tradition. (Two essays from the Westminster section—J. Gresham Machen and Cornelius Van Til—have been included with Princeton theology and Dutch schools respectively.) To each volume is appended George Marsden's introduction, and to each is added a bibliography, which was not in the original edition. I wish to thank James Bratt (the Dutch schools), William Yount (the Southern tradition), and Mark Noll (the Princeton theology) for their excellent work.

These three studies will be of particular interest to those who identify themselves with these traditions. I hope, however, that in addition to this anticipated readership there will be many others who look with fresh interest on these works. Those who care about the church, who treat their faith with seriousness, and who long that God's greatness, his sufficiency, and his glory would be more widely owned and celebrated, can only watch the current developments in the evangelical world with growing disquiet. Evangelical faith is showing too many signs of having become secularized, of fragmenting, of regressing to a stage of immaturity that surely raises the question as to how long it can survive as recognizably evangelical in the midst of the furnace of modernity. In the Reformation traditions there is a strength, a virility, a power of correction that needs to be heard again in today's evangelical world, and it is my prayer that in some small way these volumes may contribute to that end.

D.F.W.
Easter, 1989

INTRODUCTION: REFORMED AND AMERICAN

GEORGE M. MARSDEN

WHAT sense does it make in late twentieth-century America to talk about being "Reformed"? For most Americans the word conveys no clear meaning. Very few would think of it as a religious designation at all, and most of those would think it referred to Judaism. Even if, as in the present work, we limit the audience to those who have some notion of "Reformed theology," we are left with the problem that even among such a select group, "Reformed" has numerous differing connotations. In the United States alone there are about a dozen Reformed denominations and perhaps another half-dozen with a Reformed heritage. Within each of the Reformed denominations varieties of meanings are given to being "Reformed." These may reflect European traditions, such as Scottish or Dutch, or continental neoorthodox, as well as a variety of American developments. Each such type includes differing subtypes. For instance, within the Reformed Church in America alone, ten distinct approaches to the Reformed faith have been identified.[1] Differences across denominational lines may be sharper. A strictly confessional member of the Reformed Presbyterian Church in North America (Covenanters) might be most unhappy with the preaching at Robert Schuller's Crystal Cathedral. A fundamentalist Bible Presbyterian would refuse fellowship with almost any member of the United Church of Christ. And within most of the larger Reformed denominations, conservatives and progressives are locked in intense struggles over the true meaning of the faith.

A major purpose of this essay is to cut through the bewildering confusion of the many meanings of "Reformed" by reducing the categories to the three major Reformed emphases that have flourished in the American cultural setting. Not every Reformed heritage can be subsumed under these categories and the categories are ideal types or models rather than fully nuanced representations of the growth of each type. Nonetheless, these are the major subgroups that have been prominent among the Reformed throughout American history. So if we understand something of these three developments and emphases we can gain a fairly good picture of the main varieties of being "Reformed" in the American cultural setting.

Perhaps an illustration from my own experience can make clear the characters of the differences among these major American Reformed traditions. Most of my life I have lived in one or the other of two communities that placed great merit on being Reformed. The central meaning of "Reformed," however, has differed greatly in these two communions. The Orthodox Presbyterians, among whom I was reared, meant by "Reformed" strict adherence to Christian doctrine as contained in the infallible Scriptures and defined by the standards of the Westminster Assembly. Only Christians whose creeds were fully compatible with Westminster's and who viewed subscription to them as paramount were fully within the pale. Other factors were important to Christian life, especially a proper emphasis on the law of God as the central organizing principle in the Westminster formulations. But the operative test for "Reformed" was, with this important practical proviso, always doctrinal.

In the other community in which I have spent many years, the progressive wing of the conservative Christian Reformed Church, being "Reformed" is also taken seriously, but with very different meaning. There, a "Reformed" Christian is one who has a certain view of the relationship of Christianity to culture. She or he must affirm the lordship of Christ over all reality, see Christian principles as applicable to all areas of life, and view every calling as sacred. Although subscription to the authority of the Bible and classic Reformed creeds is significant in this community, the stronger operative test for admission is support for separate Christian schools at all levels (except, oddly, the graduate university), where the "Reformed" world-and-life view can be exemplified and taught.

I have also spent some time at institutions of mainstream American evangelicalism, such as Trinity Evangelical Divinity School and Fuller Theological Seminary, where one finds still another meaning to being "Reformed." In this context being "Reformed" must be understood in the framework of being "evangelical." "Evangelical" is a word with a more elusive meaning than "Reformed." Basically it refers to anyone who promotes proclamation of the gospel of salvation through the atoning work of Christ and has a traditional high view of Scripture alone as authority. Evangelicalism is thus much larger than just the Reformed tradition. Within American evangelicalism, however, there is an important subgroup that might be called "card-carrying" evangelicals.[2] These are persons who think of themselves primarily as "evangelicals" and who, as such, identify at least as much with evangelicalism as a movement as with their own formal denomination. Billy Graham, *Christianity*

Today, Eternity, Inter-Varsity Christian Fellowship, Wheaton College and its imitators, and seminaries such as Trinity, Fuller, and Gordon-Conwell have been prototypes of this influential interdenominational evangelicalism.

In this evangelical fellowship the dominant theological tradition is Reformed. It is by no means, however, the only tradition. One trait of this type of being "Reformed," unlike the other two, is that it is tolerant of diversity to the point of keeping close fellowship with persons of other traditions. The operative tests for fellowship among the Reformed in such communities are those of the broader American evangelical-pietist tradition—a certain style of emphasis on evangelism, personal devotions, Methodist mores, and openness in expressing one's evangelical commitment. To be "Reformed" in this setting means to find in Reformed theology the most biblical and healthiest expression of evangelical piety.

The differing emphases of these three communities suggest that in America there are at least three major meanings to being "Reformed." There are, of course, also a number of other Reformed traditions and styles in America. These include the southern, ethnically and racially defined groups, smaller denominations, progressive Reformed in mainline denominations, and some neoorthodox. Nonetheless, the three we have begun with suggest classically distinct types of emphasis that give us some working categories. Many of the developments of America's Reformed groups can be understood as variations on these typical themes.

For convenience' sake, we shall designate these three types as doctrinalist, culturalist, and pietist.[3] In doing so, it is important to remark again that the terminology refers to "ideal types" or descriptive models emphasizing one dominant trait. In reality all three groups typically embody the traits dominant among the other two. Thus a "pietist" is not typically a person who is lax in doctrine or lacking in cultural concern. Similarly, to call people doctrinalists or culturalists does not imply lack of the other two traits.

The Puritan Stock

The oldest major Reformed community in America was the Puritan, which combined strong elements of each of these emphases. Stress on strict Calvinism helped distinguish these early American settlers from their Arminian Anglican opponents. And Reformed orthodoxy was retained in most New England pulpits for at least a century and a half, to the time of the Revolution.[4] Puritans were also characterized by intense piety, often keeping close records of their spiritual health. Moreover, New England's Puritans were America's most successful Reformed culture builders. Virtually free from outside control during their formative first half-century, they built the closest thing humanly possible to their conception of a biblical kingdom. This impressive effort had a lasting impact on the ideals of American civilization. It is ironic that "Reformed" has so little meaning in America today when in fact the culture has been so shaped by that heritage.

The lasting culture-shaping impact of seventeenth-century Puritanism is rivaled by the long-term influence of its eighteenth-century style of piety, epitomized by the Great Awakening. The eighteenth century was generally an era of widespread resurgent pietism, emphasizing personal commitment to the Savior more than Christian culture building. The Great Awakening in New England was part of a wider Protestant pietist awakening that had begun in Germany and spread to most of the Protestant world. In England its largest manifestation was in Methodism. In America it appeared first primarily as pietist revivalism in Reformed churches.

At the height of the first surge of the Great Awakening in America, around 1740, the classic patterns of American Reformed divisions began to emerge. By this time the other major Reformed group, the Scotch-Irish and Scottish Presbyterian, was on the scene. The often changing relations of the Scottish churches to the state, and the sometimes troubled colonial experiences of the Scotch-Irish in the north of Ireland, fostered among Presbyterians in America varieties of views, or perhaps an ambivalence, concerning culture shaping. They inherited the Calvinist impulse to establish a Christian commonwealth; but they also had enough experience of religious oppression to be suspicious of religious establishments, especially when they were living, as in America, under British rule. The Christian commonwealth would be built by persuasion and education.[5]

The symbol of Presbyterian distinctiveness and unity was thus not a social-political program (except that they were militantly anti-British during the Revolution) but doctrinal orthodoxy. Strict confessionalism was a major trait of the largest party of Scotch-Irish and Scottish Presbyterians from their first appearance in the colonies. Presbyterianism in America, however, was from the outset fed by some other streams, not of Scottish but of English origin. English Presbyterianism itself had become tolerant of doctrinal diversity by the early eighteenth century. More importantly, New England Puritans, especially those in Connecticut, viewed themselves as close allies of Presbyterianism in the Middle Colonies and in the early eighteenth century were providing the newly formed (ca. 1706) Presbyterian Church with personnel and leaders. By the time of the Great Awakening, the New England party was closely linked with the more pietistic revivalist group of the Presbyterians. In

1741 this revivalist "New Side" group split from the antirevivalist Scotch-Irish or Scottish "Old Side."

Remarkably, these two Presbyterian "sides" reunited in 1758, thus suggesting that pietist revivalism and doctrinalist confessionalism were compatible. But the tension between these two emphases repeatedly reemerged. The classic instance was in the Old School/New School schism of 1837-38, in many ways a repetition of the Old Side/New Side conflict. The Old School was clearly the stronghold of Scotch-Irish and Scottish elements and found its unity in strict confessionalism. The New School, on the other hand, represented an alliance of more strongly pietist or prorevivalist Presbyterians with New England Congregationalists.

The Growth of Reformed Branches

By this time, however, a number of other issues surrounded this renewed confrontation between confessionalist and pietist axes. The New School was the more typically American of the two groups, its distinctive characteristics reflecting the tendencies of the ethos of the dominant American evangelicalism. This meant that they were more tolerant of theological innovation and variety than had been their predecessors in the seventeenth- and eighteenth-century American Reformed camps. This doctrinal latitude, however, was not a liberalism that involved intentional concessions to secularism (as in later modernism). Rather, it was an outgrowth of pietist zeal for revivalism. In politically liberal America, such zeal translated into some mildly anti-Calvinist (or semi-Pelagian) doctrines emphasizing an unaided human ability voluntarily to accept the revivalists' gospel message with its culminating summons of "choose ye this day." Such doctrinal innovations were held more closely in check by the New School Presbyterians than by their revivalist Congregationalist allies, such as Charles G. Finney. Moreover, they propounded these innovations in the name of greater faithfulness to Scripture alone, as opposed to what some saw as an unhealthly traditionalism of the Old School.

Openness to practical innovation also characterized the New School pietist strand of the heritage. Finney's "New Measures" for promoting revival in the manner of the high-pressure salesman were only the most prominent examples of evangelicalism's openness to departures from tradition. The spread of gospel music perhaps best exemplified the new evangelical style. Especially notable was a new emphasis on personal experience. Controversial also among the Presbyterians was the New School enthusiasm for working through ecclesiastically independent societies (what are now called parachurch agencies) for missions, evangelism, publication, education, and social reform.

This latter issue of social reform was creating a new source of controversy concerning what it meant to be "Reformed," a debate over what we are calling its culturalist heritage. Prior to the nineteenth century, questions concerning social reform had not been conspicuous, divisive issues. Until that time almost all the Reformed groups seem to have been working on the basis of a vaguely formulated, but deeply entrenched, tradition that, ideally, the religion of a nation should be exclusively Reformed. So they assumed that being Reformed accordingly involved transforming the moral ethos and legal system of a people so that it should comport with God's law. The Puritans, as we have seen, worked these principles out most fully in practice. By the early nineteenth century, however, these Reformed principles had to be translated to fit a pluralistic and democratic situation. The question therefore became that of how much emphasis the Reformed Churches should put on shaping the legal structures of a society they did not otherwise control. Was it not the case that the true mission of the church was to proclaim a pure gospel and be a model moral subcommunity within the larger community, leavening it rather than attempting to legislate morality for all?

Finding answers to these questions was complicated by the fact that sometimes the resolution to moral issues could have as much to do with where one stood politically as it did what theological principles one held. Thus, whereas regarding Sabbath observance most nineteenth-century Reformed groups could unite in supporting legislation, on the issue of slavery they were sharply divided. Moreover, opinions on the slavery issue varied strikingly with geography. In the deep South, Reformed people were adamantly opposed to any interference with the practice of black slavery and emphasized aspects of the tradition that favored confining the activities of the church to strictly "spiritual" issues. In New England, by contrast, Reformed Christians often took the lead in insisting that the churches should unrelentingly urge the state to enact immediate emancipation. In the upper South and the lower North, opinions were more varied and often more nuanced. New School Presbyterian leaders, having New England connections, were typically moderate antislavery types, while the Old School sided with the theologically conservative South in wanting to sidestep this and other social reform issues.

"Old School" and "New School" outlooks had thus emerged as the two leading American patterns of being Reformed. The Old School was most characteristically doctrinalist, while the more innovative New School combined pietist revivalism with a culturalist emphasis, inherited from the Puritans, looking for a Christianization of American life. These divisions were not confined to Presbyterians, although they took their clearest shape among them. A number of smaller denominations, including some Baptists, were strictly Reformed doctrinalist groups. Other groups, among whom were some Baptists, the Reformed Church in America, and especially the majority of New England's Congregationalists, were clearly in the New School camp and part of the Reformed wing of the formidable American evangelical coalition that stressed pietism and culturalism. Through the Civil War era, these two schools of Reformed were not irreconcilable, especially once the slavery issue was removed. Most notably, after the war, in 1869 the New School and Old School Presbyterians in the North reunited.

The South, on the other hand, remained separate, holding on to its predominantly Old School tradition and urging the church to stay out of politics. Ironically this apolitical stance of the southern church was deeply mixed with defense of the southern way of life. Accordingly, during the next century the Old School doctrinalism of the Southern Presbyterians was associated with (at least local) cultural influence. In the North, on the other hand, confessionalism lost much of its social base and became more and more associated with a remnant mentality.

The New School heritage, on the other hand, emerged by the end of the century as the stronger of the two traditions in the North. The New School, however, was a combination of two emphases, pietist and culturalist, and these were separable. The divorce between them occurred under the pressures associated with the rapid modernization and secularization of American life between 1870 and 1930. Industrialization, urbanization, immigration, and pluralization undermined the social basis for the old evangelical (and often Reformed) religious quasi-establishment. Moreover, liberal democratic ideology, emphasizing human freedom, ability, and essential goodness, undermined the distinctly Calvinist doctrines. Even more basically, the new naturalistic science and history of the day challenged the authority of the Bible.

Broadly considered, evangelical Christians who responded to these crises moved in one of two directions. One group adjusted to modern times by toning down the supernaturalistic aspects of the gospel and stressing rather those parts of the Christian message that could be realized by developing natural (although God-given) human individual or cultural potentials. On the other side, conservatives reemphasized the fundamentals of the faith, which stressed God's supernatural interventions into history. Thus in the Reformed communities, as in many other areas of American life, a new division was superimposed on existing patterns.

The modernist accommodations to prevailing ideas and ideals fit least well with doctrinalist emphases and best with culturalist. Such theological liberalism was in principle compatible with some pietist emphases (as in a romantic religion of the heart), but in the long run piety proved difficult to sustain from generation to generation without a strong sense of radical divine intervention.

In the New School traditions (including Presbyterian, Congregationalist, Reformed Church in America, Baptist, and other heirs of the nineteenth-century evangelical mainstream), where doctrinalism was not especially strong, the new liberalism flourished, at least among some of the denominational leadership. It grew first, in the late Victorian era, as a version of evangelical romantic piety. In the progressive era, following the turn of the century, it also blossomed as part of the theological basis for the social gospel movement. By this time liberal Protestantism was moving away from crucial parts of traditional evangelical doctrine, repudiating emphases on personal salvation through trust in Christ's work of substitutionary atonement and rejecting the infallibility and reliability of Scripture. These liberal notions alarmed some of the heirs to revivalist pietism. Ecclesiastical warfare broke out and eventually brought a long series of splits between the two camps. Since the social gospel was associated with the modernist tendencies, the "fundamentalist" opponents tended to reject all "social gospels," or culturalist emphases. Such rejections, however, were seldom consistently sustained. New School revivalists also had a heritage of aspiring to Christianize America on a voluntary basis. Thus even when, especially after about 1920, fundamentalists decried the social gospel, they typically still endorsed a politically conservative culturalism that involved efforts to return America to nineteenth-century evangelical standards, as was seen in the anti-evolution and prohibition movements.

The supernaturalist or fundamentalist party among the Reformed included major elements of Old School or doctrinalist heritage as well as the successors to New School evangelicalism. The Old School party, centered first at Princeton Theological Seminary and after 1929 at Westminster Theological Seminary, provided intellectual foundations for defending the traditional faith. The common enemy, modernism, brought these strict confessionalists into close alliance with Reformed people of more New School or pietist-revivalist heritage for a time. Thus by the early 1930s the strictly confessionalist Presbyterians who followed New Testament scholar and apologist J. Gresham Machen were closely allied with Presbyterians among the more strictly revivalist fundamentalists, such as those at Wheaton College or Moody Bible Institute.

The groupings among these theologically Reformed fundamentalists were complicated by the presence of still another major new camp— the dispensationalists. Dispensationalism was essentially Reformed in its nineteenth-century origins and had in later nineteenth-century America spread most among revival-oriented Calvinists. Strict Old School confessionalists were, however, uneasy with dispensationalists' separation of the Old Testament dispensation of Law from the era of Grace in the church age. Dispensationalism, accordingly, was accepted most readily by Reformed Christians who had a more New School, or revivalist-evangelical, emphasis than among the various Old School, or doctrinalist, groups. During the fundamentalist controversies, however, these two groups were thrown into each other's arms.

The union, however, did not last. In 1937 the followers of Machen who had just left the Presbyterian Church in the U.S.A. split roughly into Old School and New School camps, with the more revivalist group, led by Carl McIntire, favoring dispensationalism and total abstinence from alcoholic beverages. About the same time, doctrinalist Southern Presbyerians took a stand against dispensationalism in their denomination.

Another, less separatist branch of the New School evangelical party survived well in the "new evangelicalism" that grew out of fundamentalism after World War II. The new evangelicals were largely Reformed in leadership and had moved away from strict dispensationalism. Institutionally they gained strength at centers such as Wheaton College, Fuller Theological Seminary, Trinity Evangelical Divinity School, and Gordon-Conwell Theological Seminary. *Christianity Today*, founded in 1956 under the editorship of Carl F. H. Henry, gave them wide visibility and influence. Inter-Varsity Christian Fellowship, InterVarsity Press, and the ministry of Francis Schaeffer also added substantially to the outreach of this Reformed evangelicalism. Keeping cordial relations with many individuals and groups not Reformed and with evangelicals both within and outside mainline denominations, this New School tradition has emerged as one of the most influential expressions of evangelicalism today.

The Old School, though smaller, also remains active. It has wide influence through Westminster Theological Seminary and similar conservative schools. Denominationally, it is especially strong in the Presbyterian Church of America and in the conservative wing of the Christian Reformed Church. It is also found among Reformed Baptists and in other smaller Reformed denominations.

Of the three strands of the heritage, the culturalist emphasis is the least unified today. Nonetheless, it is perhaps as prominent as it ever has been. This continuing emphasis, that Calvinists should be transforming culture and bringing all of creation back to its proper relationship to God's law, has been resurgent due to the convergence of a number of developments. Most clearly articulating these views have been the North American Kuyperians, followers of the turn-of-the-century Dutch theologian and politician, Abraham Kuyper. Kuyperianism was brought to America largely by the Dutch-American Christian Reformed Church, where a hard-line Kuyperianism also developed among the admirers of

Dutch philosopher Herman Dooyeweerd. Dooyeweerdianism has enlisted non-Dutch disciples, but the widest influence of Kuyperianism spread in a mild form through the neoevangelical movement after World War II. The fundamentalist tradition, said neoevangelical spokespersons such as Carl F. H. Henry, had not sufficiently recognized that the Christian task involves relating a Christian "World-and-life view" to all of culture and politics.[6]

By the 1970s such moderately conservative emphases were converging with the resurgence of conservative politics among American fundamentalists and fundamentalistic evangelicals. Fundamentalists had their own, vaguely Reformed, traditions of wanting to Christianize America. Versions of Kuyperian Calvinism such as those suggested by Francis Schaeffer in the influential political ministry of his later years helped articulate the new fundamentalist conservative political emphases of the Moral Majority. Schaeffer drew many of his political ideas from the work of the politically conservative Dooyeweerdian thinker, Rousas J. Rushdoony. Rushdoony also contributed to the emergence of the hyper-Reformed "theonomist" movement, which insists that Old Testament law should be the basis of American civil law.

The irony in this resurgence of Reformed culturalism is that the culturalists, who are often united in theological theory, are so deeply divided in practice. Cutting across the culturalist movement is a seemingly insurmountable divide between those who are politically conservative and those who are politically liberal. Many of the American followers of Kuyper have been politically liberal and these had an impact on the politically progressive evangelicalism that emerged during the 1960s and early 1970s.[7] Moreover, the politically liberal Reformed culturalist camp includes Reformed Christians in mainline denominations whose traditions still reflect the political progressivism of the social gospel days. In addition, the neoorthodox heritage in such denominations has contributed, especially via the work of H. Richard Niebuhr and Reinhold Niebuhr, to generally Reformed culturalist sensibilities tempered by a Lutheran sense of the ambiguities inherent in relating Christianity to an essentially pagan culture.

The American Reformed community today, then, still includes substantial representation of the three classic emphases, doctrinalism, pietism, and culturalism. These three are, of course, not incompatible and the unity of Reformed Christians in America would be much greater were this compatibility recognized and emphasized.

The question of unity, however, is complicated by the twentieth-century divisions of modernists and fundamentalists that have cut across the traditional divisions. Neoorthodox and dispensationalist variations add further complications. Moreover, among those who are primarily culturalists, conflicting political allegiances subvert Reformed unity. Nonetheless, there remain a substantial number of Reformed Christians whose faith reflects a balance, or potential balance, of the three traditional emphases. It is these Christians who need to find each other and who might benefit from reflecting on what it should mean to be Reformed.

They can also learn from considering the characteristic weaknesses, as well as the strengths, of their tradition. Perhaps the greatest fault of American Reformed communities since Puritan times is that they have cultivated an elitism. Ironically, the doctrine of election has been unwittingly construed as meaning that Reformed people have been endowed with superior theological, spiritual, or moral merit by God himself. The great irony of this is that the genius of the Reformed faith has been its uncompromising emphasis on God's grace, with the corollary that our own feeble efforts are accepted, not because of any merit, but solely due to God's grace and Christ's work. The doctrine of grace, then, ought to cultivate humility as a conspicuous trait of Reformed spirituality. A strong sense of our own inadequacies is an important asset for giving us positive appreciation of those who differ from us.

Yet too often Reformed people have been so totally confident of their own spiritual insights that they have been unable to accept or work with fellow Reformed Christians whose emphases may vary slightly. Perhaps some review of the rich varieties of theological views among the Reformed in America today will contribute to bringing tolerance and search for balance. Moreover, the unmistakable minority status of the "Reformed" in America today should help foster the need for mutual understanding and respect. Above all, however, a revival of the central Reformed distinctive—the sense of our own unworthiness and of total dependence on God's grace, as revealed especially through Christ's sacrificial work—should bring together many who in late twentieth-century America still find it meaningful to say "I am Reformed."

Notes: Reformed and American

1. I. John Hesselink, *On Being Reformed: Distinctive Characteristics and Common Misunderstandings* (Ann Arbor: Servant Books, 1983), 2 and 113.

2. This concept is elaborated in *Evangelicalism and Modern America,* ed. George M. Marsden (Grand Rapids: Wm. B. Eerdmans Publishing Company, 1984).

3. These categories are roughly those suggested by Nicholas Wolterstorff, "The AACS in the CRC," *The Reformed Journal* 24 (December 1974): 9-16.

4. Harry S. Stout, *The New England Soul: Preaching and Religious Culture in Colonial New England* (New York: Oxford University Press, forthcoming).

5. The Reformed efforts to build a Christian culture are well described in Fred J. Hood, *Reformed America: The Middle and Southern States, 1783-1837* (University, AL: University of Alabama Press, 1980).

6. Carl F. H. Henry, *The Uneasy Conscience of Modern Fundamentalism* (Grand Rapids: Wm. B. Eerdmans Publishing Company, 1947), 10.

7. See Robert Booth Fowler, *A New Engagement: Evangelical Political Thought, 1966-1976* (Grand Rapids: Wm. B. Eerdmans Publishing Company, 1982), for an account of this relationship and other developments in evangelical political thought.

1

THE PRINCETON THEOLOGY

MARK A. NOLL

Archibald Alexander

A. A. Hodge

THE Princeton Theology was a distinctly American and a distinctly nineteenth-century expression of classical Reformed faith. Misunderstanding results if we regard it either as a simple restatement of Augustinian Calvinism, untouched by its surroundings, or as a simple product of American culture, haphazardly garnished with traditional Reformed words. During the nineteenth century—which in America may be regarded as that period stretching from the inspiring moments of the Revolution to the disillusionments of World War I—the Princeton theologians functioned as a loyal opposition. On the basis of their Calvinism, they questioned American myths about the power of the self, the American trust in consciousness, the American rejection of the past, and the American idolization of democracy. Yet they also took their stand as cultural insiders. They spoke Calvinism with an unmistakable American accent. With most other intellectuals of their day, they relied on a Common Sense approach to truth, they assumed the value-free character of scientific investigation, they were suspicious of high-flown ideas from the continent, and they took economic and political self-reliance for granted. The men who articulated the Princeton Theology, the convictions that constituted it, and the institutions in which it took shape were much more than functions of nineteenth-century American culture. But neither were they ever less than that. This paper attempts to place these men, convictions, and institutions in proper context before making an assessment of this important theological school, both in comparison to other varieties of Reformed faith and with regard to its relevance today.[1]

Men

Of the many individuals who contributed to the Princeton Theology during its long life from the founding of a Presbyterian seminary at Princeton, New Jersey, in 1812, to the reorganization of that institution

in 1929, three were clearly most important: Archibald Alexander, founding professor; his pupil, Charles Hodge; and Benjamin Breckinridge
Warfield, who in his turn had studied under Hodge.

Archibald Alexander's experience before coming to Princeton and
his initial leadership of the seminary set the course that his successors
followed.[2] Alexander (1772-1851) arrived at Princeton in 1812 after a full
career as revivalist, educator, pastor, and theologian. During the 1780s
and 1790s he witnessed and led revivals in his native Virginia. As a
result he remained more disposed to value "enthusiastic" religion than
was normally the case at Princeton. Yet even as he took part in the practical renewal of the church, he was also putting his mind to use. Alexander studied privately with the Rev. William Graham, one of the most
ardent disciples of John Witherspoon, then president of Princeton College. What Graham taught Alexander especially was to think for himself,
to distrust learned authorities in favor of the testimony of his own experience. Alexander, however, soon went beyond Graham's instruction
to embrace as well major expressions of historic Calvinism. Early in his
ministry he eagerly read Jonathan Edwards, especially Edwards's treatment of the will. Alexander later worked through several seventeenth-
century Reformed dogmaticians for his own benefit. When he came to
Princeton, after service as a pastor in Virginia and Philadelphia and a
stint as president of Hampden-Sydney College, he carried the intellectual resources and the practical concerns that would mark that seminary
long after his passing.

Charles Hodge (1797-1878) and B. B. Warfield (1851-1921) receive
separate treatment in this book, so it is not necessary to outline their
careers here.[3] Suffice it to say that Hodge fleshed out the framework
Alexander had established in a wide-ranging collection of works: exegetical commentaries, popular exhortation, denominational history, lectures, and eventually a massive textbook in systematic theology, but
above all polemical periodical essays. Although not as comfortable with
revivalistic piety as Alexander nor as technically brilliant as Warfield,
Hodge was the most complex of the major Princeton theologians. He
succeeded in bringing together more elements from the Reformed heritage, American culture, and pastoral concern than anyone in the tradition. Warfield, for his part, faced a different range of challenges than his
predecessors, including wholesale intellectual defalcation from the evangelical Protestantism that was a cultural given in the America of Alexander and Hodge. Warfield set himself to expose the fallacies of modern
alternatives to historic Christianity, a task that he carried out in hundreds
of essays and thousands of reviews. His mind was discriminating, and
his heart was faithful to historic Calvinism. Warfield did not have the

same pastoral or ecclesiastical instincts as Alexander or Hodge, but he was no less a warrior for the convictions that they held dear.

A. A. Hodge (1823-1886), who taught at Princeton for ten years between the old age of his father and his own death, heads the second rank of Princeton theologians. He was a master of summation and popular presentation, rather than of the polemics that Charles Hodge and Warfield mastered. In this regard his service resembled that of many other Princetonians who augmented and expanded the major insights of Alexander, Hodge, and Warfield, including especially James Waddel Alexander (1804-1859) and Joseph Addison Alexander (1809-1860), sons of the founder who carried out a myriad of intellectual and practical services to the Presbyterian Church, Princeton College, and the seminary; Lyman Atwater (1813-1883), a transplanted New Englander who shouldered the major burden in replying to the theological errors that Princetonians perceived in his native region; William Henry Green (1825-1900), a professor of Old Testament who held firmly to traditional ideas about the Bible even while he appreciated new scholarship on the Middle East; and J. Gresham Machen (1881-1937), a New Testament scholar who led a remnant of the Princeton Theology out into the wilderness after the directors of the seminary altered its course in 1929.[4]

The leaders who formulated the Princeton Theology were men of intelligence, theological insight, pastoral concern, and practical wisdom. Yet what set them apart in their day, and what makes them intriguing objects of inquiry after their passing, is the beliefs they held, the methods they used to propagate those beliefs, and their efforts to preserve them for later generations.

Convictions

The Princeton Theology was not as simple as either proponents or opponents liked to make it. Princetonians sometimes spoke of themselves as Francis Landy Patton did in 1912 at the seminary's centennial: they "simply taught the old Calvinistic theology without modification." Those who doubt the wisdom of Old Princeton sometimes perceive an equally simple, if contrasting picture. One of these was Frank Hugh Foster who, writing of Charles Hodge as representative of the school, suggested in 1907 that Hodge "may be safely left by the historian of a progressive school of theology to the natural consequence of his own remark that during the many years of his predominance at Princeton that institution had never brought forward a single original thought."[5]

The reality was something different. Princeton did maintain a Reformed position in continuity with previous generations of Calvinistic theologians. But the Princetonians did not always organize their efforts, or emphasize the same relationships, as their Reformed predecessors had. Old Princeton often took procedural and methodological questions for granted, even when these exerted considerable influence on the shape of its thought. In these and other ways the theology that developed at Princeton was as complex as that of any of the other major bodies of Christian thought in nineteenth-century America. The strengths and complexity of Princeton stand out more clearly in an examination of those convictions that were most important to the school.

1. *Reformed Confessionalism.* "Calvinism," wrote Warfield in 1904, "is just religion in its purity. We have only, therefore, to conceive of religion in its purity, and that is Calvinism."[6] The Princetonians would no doubt have been distressed had they known that theologians in the late twentieth century would study them primarily in regard to their technical views on the Bible or for their use of the Scottish Philosophy of Common Sense. While they certainly held firm views on Scripture and philosophy, these matters were parts of a larger enterprise, to proclaim the dignity, necessity, and cogency of the Reformed faith. Warfield's words spoke for them all.

Princeton theologians freely employed the riches of the Calvinist heritage in setting out their own faith, although they did not draw equally from all varieties of Reformed tradition. Charles Hodge, for example, admired both the Thirty-Nine Articles of the Church of England and the Heidelberg Catechism, but seems to have made slight use in his *Systematic Theology* either of these documents or of the theological traditions they represent. Yet their wide-ranging use of Augustine on salvation, of Calvin, of several major Puritans, of Luther and orthodox Lutherans, of the Westminster standards, and of Swiss dogmaticians after Calvin suggests the breadth of their Reformed commitments.

The winsome proclamation of this Calvinism was the heart of their concern. Nowhere was Charles Hodge more eloquent than when defending Reformed views of human nature or of divine sovereignty in salvation—as, for example, in polemics directed at Charles Finney or the New Haven Theology of Nathaniel W. Taylor. Warfield was constrained to write scores of articles upholding a broadly orthodox view of the Bible's inspiration, but he wrote even more on specifically Reformed concerns: defending Calvinistic views of revelation (against evangelical perfectionists as well as against Catholics and modernists), offering the views of Calvin and Augustine for modern inspection, and detailing the intended purposes of the Westminster divines.

Princeton Calvinism shared the main emphases of the Reformed tradition: The Fall perverted a perfect creation, led to divine condemnation, and established human guilt. Adam's sin was imputed to all humans, who properly deserve the condemnation which that sinfulness entails. The same process of imputation that rendered humanity doomed in Adam justified the elect through faith in Christ. God expressed his saving purposes in covenanting to offer salvation through Christ. Sinners, turned from God by rebellious natures, were "bound" to their own sinful desires until God changed their hearts through Scripture, Christian nurture, preaching, and the sacraments. Redeemed sinners, though hamstrung by the lingering effects of the Fall, yet were fitted by the Holy Spirit for fruitful service in the Kingdom of God. These principles made up the solid core of Princeton belief to which all other major concerns were attendant.

Questions do remain, however, about the nature of Princeton's Reformed faith. The school tended to assume that positions drawn from various Reformed sources, shaped by the questions of the nineteenth century, and applied in modern polemics were simple restatements of an undifferentiated Reformed orthodoxy. In other words, Princetonians regarded theology as a static entity not affected to any appreciable degree by historical development. Arguments first made by Augustine against Pelagius, by Calvin against the Council of Trent, or by Francis Turretin against his opponents in the late seventeenth century were, to them, parts of one dogmatic whole. They did not consider the possibility that previous Reformed theologians may have individualized aspects of the biblical revelation even as they put the Scriptures to use in their respective eras.

This relative lack of sensitivity to historical conditioning, much more than a supposedly servile use of Turretin, is the most important question concerning the place of Princeton in the history of Reformed thought.[7] No doubt can exist that they were important spokesmen for that tradition. Some doubt may arise as to whether they always represented the tradition to its best advantage. The Princeton assumption that it was possible simply to restate tested and true positions for the present arose from both their confidence in the truth-telling character of Scripture and their particular beliefs in philosophy and science, convictions that deserve individual attention in any overview of their theology.

2. *Scripture.* From first to last the Princeton theologians held to a high view of the Bible's inspiration and authority. At his inaugural in 1812, Alexander preached on John 5:39, "Search the Scriptures," in order to establish the Bible as the foundation for the seminary's existence.[8] In 1915 Warfield summed up a lifetime's work on the same subject by contending in a magisterial interpretation of "Inspiration" that "the Scriptures are throughout a Divine book, created by the Divine energy and speaking in their every part with Divine authority directly to the heart

of the readers."[9] This conviction undergirded the long history of the theology.

Charles Hodge was called upon to make the first major restatements of Alexander's views on Scripture as the claims of Higher Criticism began to enter the United States at mid-century. Yet even in his *Systematic Theology*, which was finally published in 1872-73, Hodge offered his teaching on Scripture mostly as a corrective to deficient positions that he had encountered early in the century, especially those of Roman Catholics and subjectivist pietists. It fell to his son and Warfield to scrutinize the new criticism more thoroughly. They did this most completely in a memorable essay published in 1881, entitled simply "Inspiration," in which they upheld the church's historic confidence in the letter as well as the spirit of the Scriptures, described presuppositions on both sides of the contemporary discussion, and contended for the traditional view on the basis of the Bible's own testimony concerning itself.[10] In later essays Warfield explored numerous facets of the issue, laying especially heavy emphasis on the way in which the Bible's inspiration did not detract from its character as a thoroughly human (though errorless) book. Princeton's fidelity to the plenary inspiration of the Bible was consistent; each generation refined the position that it had received. The effort throughout was painstaking, careful, scholarly, and learned.

The Princeton adherence to strict views of inspiration does not, however, answer every important question one can ask about Scripture. Why, for instance, should we believe the Bible and a biblical faith? Charles Hodge sometimes said, as in quoting a German source in 1840: "Faith is no work of reason, and therefore cannot be overthrown by it, since believing no more arises from arguments than tasting or seeing."[11] Alexander and Warfield were more likely to suggest that irrefragable testimony and close logic can demonstrate that the Bible is God's word and that we should base our faith on that reasonable certainty.[12] Or again, why do the Princeton theologians usually act as if the Bible existed primarily for the formulation of dogma? As George Marsden points out in this book, other Reformed communities, though not despising dogma, have used the Scriptures as much to inspire piety or guide cultural reformation. For their part, the Princeton theologians usually considered biblical piety a strict product of correct biblical dogma. And they were largely silent about the Bible's potential for cultural reformation.[13] Yet rarely did Princetonians reflect directly on their preference for a dogmatic approach to Scripture.[14] A further question concerns relationships between the "book of God" and the "book of nature." Charles Hodge felt that ideas of design, which he found in Scripture, negated Darwinism. A. A. Hodge and Warfield, on the other hand, both felt that the Bible could be read in such a way as to make peace with Darwinism.[15]

To summarize, the Princeton teaching on the nature of Scripture was consistent and very clear: the Bible was God's written word; it was a genuine product of human activity that could be studied historically; yet the Bible was also the presentation of the most perfect truth in all that its human authors (under the inspiration of the Holy Spirit) meant to affirm; it was effective in doing the converting and sanctifying work of the Spirit. On questions about the place of the Bible in apologetics, its place in the church's life more generally, and its interpretation in relationship to general revelation (as in science), the Princeton testimony on Scripture was less unified. Such unanswered questions do not detract from their positive testimony on Scripture, but rather suggest that the many good words from Princeton on the Bible did not include the last word.

3. *Scottish Common Sense Philosophy.* Although it had long been recognized that the Scottish Philosophy of Common Sense played a leading role at Princeton, it was not until the publication of Sydney Ahlstrom's seminal essay on the general subject in 1955 that this dimension of the theology began to receive careful attention.[16] Since then it has become a commonplace to hold that Old Princeton was heavily, even uniquely, indebted to this philosophy. There are several plausible reasons for doing so.

John Witherspoon (1723-1794), the instructor of Alexander's mentor William Graham (1746-1799) at Princeton College, had trained his students in the convictions of the Scottish philosophy. And Graham was among its most ardent exponents.[17] From study with Graham, Alexander adopted many of the principles that Witherspoon brought with him to America from Scottish thinkers like Francis Hutcheson (1694-1746) and Thomas Reid (1710-1796). These philosophers were attempting to rescue the English "moderate" Enlightenment of Isaac Newton and John Locke from the skepticism of David Hume and the idealism of George Berkeley.[18] As Alexander came to express these positions, they included an affirmation that the "common sense" of humankind could verify the deliverances of the physical senses and of intuitive consciousness (i.e., the "moral sense"). It was second nature for him to think, as illustrated in his earliest lectures at the seminary and in his last, posthumously published book, that this "common sense" provided the basis for an irrefutable apologetic concerning the existence of God and the reality of biblical revelation.[19] Along with Witherspoon, Graham, and their Scottish mentors, Alexander was an enthusiast for empiricism and induction. Scrupulous investigation imitating methods of the "natural philosophers" would lead to the same kind of success in ethics and theology as the great Newton had enjoyed in studying the physical world.[20]

Charles Hodge imbibed the Scottish Philosophy from Alexander, as well as from the pastor of his youth, Ashbel Green, who became president of Princeton College in 1812, the year that Hodge began his studies there. (Green's major educational change at the college was to restore Witherspoon's lectures in moral philosophy as the integrating text for the undergraduates.) Hodge's debt to the Scottish Philosophy appears most clearly in the opening pages of his *Systematic Theology* where, in oft-quoted lines, he likened the construction of dogmatic systems to scientific exploration: "The Bible is to the theologian what nature is to the man of science. It is his store-house of facts; and his method of ascertaining what the Bible teaches is the same as that which the natural philosopher adopts to ascertain what nature teaches."[21] Warfield learned the Scottish Philosophy from James McCosh, the last prominent defender of the system, who in 1868 came from Scotland to Princeton College as Witherspoon had a century before. That was also the year in which Warfield began his undergraduate studies. Other spokesmen for the Princeton Theology asserted Common Sense convictions aggressively or, like A. A. Hodge, simply accepted them as the natural axioms for theological inquiry.

When this eighteenth-century philosophical position was added to Princeton's Reformed convictions, the result was not always propitious. Princetonians could be overconfident in assuming that the deliverances of their own consciousness equaled the common intuitions of all humanity. They were naive in thinking that chains of apologetical reasoning could begin with no moral preconditions in the seeker and no predetermined assumptions about the end of inquiry. And although their Calvinism pointed in an opposite direction, their philosophical allegiance could at times leave them sounding like scientistic positivists.

Yet this is not the whole story. Princeton's accommodation to Scottish Common Sense Philosophy was neither total nor comprehensive. While harboring few reservations about epistemological and methodological aspects of the Scottish position, they regularly resisted its ethical implications, at least on major doctrines.[22] They were not like their theological contemporaries in New England who substantially altered traditional Reformed views of human nature and divine sovereignty on the basis, in E. A. Park's words, of "the fundamental laws of human belief," those "ethical axioms, which so many fathers in the church have undervalued," which are derived from *"the philosophy of common sense."*[23] By contrast, the Princeton theologians never allowed the deliverances of refined Victorian conscience to overwhelm basic Calvinistic beliefs in human moral incapacity or to replace supreme confidence in the sometimes "unenlightened" pronouncements of the Bible.

Thus, the Princeton investment in Common Sense Philosophy did not lead to a comprehensive reordering of traditional Reformed theology as it did for N. W. Taylor. Rather Princetonians merely added Common Sense to their more traditional theological convictions. The result was a system with more internal stress and less methodological rigor than Taylor's New Haven Theology; and it was a system that did not come to terms with religious experience as forthrightly as did Horace Bushnell.[24] Yet for all these weaknesses, the very naiveté of Princeton's Common Sense convictions was a disguised blessing. Acting intuitively, Princeton made profitable conjunctions where Common Sense really did support traditional Reformed positions (as in the impossibility of living as if there were no God who maintained the physical and moral worlds). To be sure, they muddied the waters when discussing the first principles of ethics by clumsily intermingling Scottish beliefs about universal human capacities with Reformed convictions about the moral effects of the Fall.[25] But Common Sense intuitionism was never the last word, especially when it came to teachings on the sovereignty of God over human consciousness and the superiority of divine revelation to the inner voice of the self. And these were convictions that were fading during the nineteenth century almost as fast among American evangelicals at large as among the champions of the new theologies.[26]

4. *Religious Experience, The Work of the Spirit.* In spite of their reputation as scholastics or rationalists, and in spite of their fidelity to the objective works of God, the Princeton theologians constantly stressed the importance of religious experience and the need for the work of the Holy Spirit. The Sunday afternoon "conferences" with seminary students that lasted from generation to generation throughout most of the century, their occasional sermons, and especially the commentaries and selected polemical essays of Charles Hodge testify to consistent efforts at giving the supernatural work of the Spirit its proper place in the life of the individual believer and of the church as a whole.[27] As Reformed theologians, the Princetonians always insisted that the Spirit worked through "means."[28] Yet none of them neglected the importance of religious experience, even if they insisted that such experience not be opposed to the propositional testimony of Scripture and the intellectual structure of the confessions.

The pertinent question for the Princeton theologians is not whether they had a place for religious experience and the work of the Holy Spirit. As Professor Andrew Hoffecker's fine recent book makes clear beyond cavil, they certainly did.[29] The question is rather where this religious experience, where the work of the Holy Spirit, fit into their theology. It is hard to escape the conclusion that on this score, as in the Princeton appropriation of Common Sense Philosophy, no entirely satisfactory integration occurred. The Charles Hodge who laid such great store by "facts" and "scientific method" could also argue for the priority of inner convictions over external argument in the reception of religious truth. And as David Kelsey has pointed out, even Warfield, the most carefully logical of the Princeton theologians, often described his belief in Scripture as arising more from the internal power of the written word than from conclusions out of a neutral chain of argument.[30] At issue is not their seriousness about religious experience, but the incorporation of that seriousness in their theology as a whole.

The quickening power of the Holy Spirit, manifest through divinely ordained means, was a principal feature of Princeton religion. That this element of the Princeton Theology seems to stay in the background is the responsibility first of these men themselves, since they seemed less clear about the place of the Spirit's work in their theology than in their lives. But it is also a result of a historical failure to realize that occasional Princeton statements that ignore or play down the importance of religious experience were not necessarily the foundational axioms of the theology as a whole.

Institutions

The convictions of the Princeton theologians are the main reasons for their continuing importance. Yet historically considered, the institutions that embodied those beliefs were nearly as impressive as the doctrines themselves. The ideas gave the theology its direction, but the institutions made it influential in America.

Princeton Seminary, the second major American school devoted to postgraduate theological education, was, quite naturally, the place where the Princeton Theology received its fullest institutional expression. The way the seminary came into existence had more than a little influence on the course that the Princeton Theology would take.[31] The seminary was founded in 1812, five years after the establishment of Andover Seminary, in response to a feeling that America was undergoing a cultural crisis of unprecedented seriousness. Its founders—Ashbel Green and Samuel Miller as well as Alexander—had several related purposes for the school: to fit clergymen to meet the cultural crisis, to roll back what they perceived as tides of irreligion sweeping the country, and to provide a learned defense of Christianity generally and the Bible specifically. The conserving character of the institution did not change during the life of the Princeton Theology. As its centennial in 1912, the seminary had enrolled over 1,000 more students than any other theological school in the United States. A total of 6,386 students studied at Princeton from Alexander's inauguration to Warfield's death. Some of them became famous theologians, educators, and ministers in their own right (by 1912 the alumni included fifty-six moderators of General Assemblies and five bishops of the Protestant Episcopal Church). Even more impressive was the steady infusion of ministers into the ongoing congregational life of the nation, ministers exposed to a powerful expression of American Calvinism and, much more often than not, its advocates as well.

The Princeton Theology spread outward through seminary graduates, but even more visibly through the printed page. A vast cornucopia of essays, commentaries, treatises, reviews, and pamphlets—on an incredibly diverse range of topics—tumbled from the presses of Philadelphia, New York, and Princeton itself to present this theology to the public. Many of these books, like Charles Hodge's *Way of Life* and his *Systematic Theology*, or the theological compendia of A. A. Hodge, reached wide audiences throughout the nineteenth century. A remarkably large number of Princeton books remain in print to this day.

Significant as the books undoubtedly were, the Princeton Theology received its fullest expression in periodicals.[32] Their learned and extensive reviews contained the fullest exposition of Princeton positions, the most vigorous attacks on rivals, and the most thoughtful reflections on great national events and significant intellectual milestones. The greatest of these journals was Charles Hodge's *Biblical Repertory and Princeton Review*, begun in 1825 in an effort mostly to transmit European theological scholarship to America, but changed over the years, and under a series of titles, to a mighty instrument of theological instruction. Although he had assistance in editing its pages, as indicated by the long lists of articles contributed by the Alexanders, Lyman Atwater, Albert Baldwin Dod, and other stalwarts, this was the supreme vehicle for Charles Hodge's convictions.[33] After managing the review for nearly forty years, he called his labor "a ball-and-chain" borne "with scarcely any other compensation than the high privilege and honour of making it an organ for upholding sound Presbyterianism, the cause of the country, and the honour of our common Redeemer."[34] Yet even foes recognized the power of the work in the journal, like the editor of Lyman Beecher's autobiography who said it was "the most powerful organ in the land." Friendly voices were even more extravagant, like the *British Quarterly Review*, which in 1871 called Hodge's journal "beyond all question the greatest purely theological Review that has ever been published in the English tongue."[35]

What made the *Princeton Review* so powerful, and what also contributed to the influence of the journals that A. A. Hodge and B. B. Warfield managed, was the Princeton ability to enlarge a parochial controversy into a full-blown defense of Reformed doctrines. For depth of treatment, clarity of argumentation, and seriousness of purpose, there is simply nothing in twentieth-century American religious life to match the theological discussions in nineteenth-century periodicals. And the

Princeton Review took a leading role in many of these. Whether Hodge was debating the relationship between intellect and feeling with E. A. Park (7 articles, 265 pages, over 18 months, in the *Princeton Review* and Park's *Bibliotheca Sacra* during 1850-52), tilting with Horace Bushnell (three lengthy articles over a twenty-year span), or addressing more particular issues of interest only to Presbyterians, the journal demanded reading.

After Hodge's day, changes in the American academy reduced the influence of the theological journals. Still, A. A. Hodge in *The Presbyterian Review* (1880-1889) and Warfield in *The Presbyterian and Reformed Review* (1890-1902) and *The Princeton Theological Review* (1903-1921) reached nearly the same degree of seriousness and comprehension.

The final institution of the Princeton Theology was the Presbyterian Church. Although the seminary never enjoyed the confidence of the entire denomination, its influence made it a power to be reckoned with. It maintained consistent Old School views in the schism of 1837, urged caution in the reunion of the northern Old and New School denominations in 1867, arrayed itself at the turn of the twentieth century against innovation on the Confession and theological inclusiveness as a denominational strategy, and in general sought to keep the denomination close to its confessional Calvinist roots.[36] From 1835 through 1867, with but one exception, Charles Hodge reported on the year's General Assembly in the *Princeton Review*. This quickly established Hodge as one of the most visible arbiters of Presbyterian opinion in the century. "There is no inducement," one of Hodge's allies once wrote, "to prepare a good article for the July number, because every one turns at once to that on the General Assembly which absorbs all interest."[37]

The expression of Princeton convictions in these institutions—the seminary, their books and journals, the Presbyterian Church—was *the* Princeton Theology. Many convictions of Old Princeton deserve a place among the church's perpetual beliefs. But a judicious definition of this theology as a concrete historical entity must always come back to the institutions in which the Princeton beliefs took shape during the nineteenth century. To say this, however, raises the question of the Princeton Theology in relation to its times.

The Nineteenth-Century Context

Many of the supposed defects of the Princeton theologians, and some of their vaunted triumphs as well, become less striking if the work of the school is placed in its historical context. To study Princeton only in relationship to twentieth-century theological developments, or, from a different perspective, to ignore the centuries between Calvin's activity in Geneva and Alexander's in Princeton, is to short-circuit sympathetic understanding of these theologians. It may even be that the genuine contribution of the Princeton Theology will only be apparent when it is placed against the background of its times.

To do this shows immediately that much of the Princeton Theology was simply a singular expression of the ordinary affirmations of their day. For example, the Princetonians used Scottish Common Sense Philosophy mostly because it was America's common intellectual coinage of the nineteenth century. Early in the period orthodox Congregationalists at Yale as well as Unitarians at Harvard embraced this perspective nearly as enthusiastically as did Presbyterian Princeton. Common Sense assumptions later became commonplace in the theological pronouncements of an incredibly broad range of American theologians: revisionist Calvinists like N. W. Taylor, more consistent Calvinists like E. A. Park, New School Presbyterians like Albert Barnes, Disciples of Christ spokesmen like Alexander Campbell, Unitarians like Andrews Norton, and so on. At least for much of the nineteenth century, the Princetonians' Scottish Realism shows us more how they moved with their culture than against it.[38]

Once again, Princeton defended the authority of the Bible because for most of the century almost all evangelical Protestants took this for granted. In the last third of the century, the Princetonians came to stress more the cognitive than the affective veracity of Scripture. But even here the fact that these later Princeton proposals received such wide support from non-Calvinist groups would suggest that there was nothing peculiarly distinctive about the positions. And for the first two-thirds of the century, as essays by Randall Balmer and John Woodbridge have shown, it is hard to distinguish the Princeton views on the Bible from those of the American evangelical world at large.[39]

Similarly, Princetonians advocated a naive empiricism in the construction of theology because most American intellectuals approached theory-formation like this. During the nineteenth century historians, public servants, social scientists, and even artists, geniuses, and crackpots, all looked to simple scientific generalizations as the path to truth.[40] In this climate the Princeton methodological naiveté was part and parcel of a more general epistemological innocence in America.

For most of the nineteenth century, then, the Princeton theologians merely shared widespread cultural values in their convictions about the Bible, Scottish Common Sense Philosophy, and scientific empiricism. The distinctive Princeton achievement was to absorb these cultural assumptions into their Calvinism without losing that Calvinism. To be heard in the nineteenth century, it was necessary for Princeton to adopt the intellectual conventions of the day. Schools of theology that did not do this, like the Mercersberg theology of J. W. Nevin, are of considerable interest to twentieth-century scholars, but they were close to nullities in their own day. The truly remarkable thing about the work of the Princetonians was that so much historic Calvinism remained even as they adjusted their thought to accommodate American intellectual conventions.

Perspective: Princeton, Jonathan Edwards, and the Dutch

To assess the accomplishments of the Princetonians as well as their deficiencies, it is helpful to compare them with other representatives of Reformed theology. Two obvious candidates for such a task are Jonathan Edwards, who forged the most powerful engine of American Calvinism during the eighteenth century, and the Dutch followers of Abraham Kuyper, who through immigrant communities had established a presence in America by the end of the nineteenth century.

The many striking contrasts among these Reformed theologians can loom larger than their commonalities, even if their agreements were far more extensive than their disagreements. Though later theologians and historians have belabored their differences, the compliments that Princeton and the Dutch paid to Edwards and to each other were sincere.[41] The three represented different geographic regions and ethnic origins— New England from English stock, middle American from largely Scotch-Irish background, and immigrants from Holland—and they possessed very different temperaments, but the three shared a remarkable resemblance in efforts to do theology and approach life in a Calvinistic way.

Yet the differences were major. Edwards and the Dutch, first, showed much more concern for the intellectual framework of theology than did Old Princeton. The former wrestled with these questions as full-scale theological issues in their own right. Opinions differ concerning the success of these efforts, but they still resulted in a great deal of insight concerning method and a more obviously Christian grasp of procedural problems than the Princetonians displayed. By way of compensation, Princeton's relative lack of sophistication on such matters left its theology more accessible to a wide audience—at least so long as their assumptions about method corresponded roughly with those of the general populace, and that was for nearly one hundred years.

Second, the three differed in how their approach to Scripture affected their picture of the Christian's task in society. Princeton used the Bible to construct dogma, while it was content to accept the cultural conventions of the merchant-yeoman middle class without question. To Edwards the Bible was a resource for reflective piety, for discovering the divine and supernatural light that graciously converts the darkened heart; his absorption was so thorough on this theme that he seems to have given little thought to the late-Puritan society in which he lived. The Dutch, by contrast, almost defined themselves by their capacity to find scriptural principles for cultural formation, whether in education, politics, voluntary organizations, or economics. These varied uses of Scripture have appeared complementary in some circumstances and competitive in others.

Finally, the three differed in their ability to adapt to America. In spite of the combination of his genius and his piety, Edwards's Calvinism did not long survive his death. Within seventy years of his passing, "Edwardseans," though following his lead in some methodological and ethical matters, had stood on their head most of Edwards's basic affirmations about human nature, the process of salvation, and the relationship between Christ and the elect. Dutch Calvinism has sustained itself better in America, but at a price. The precepts of Kuyper and Bavinck remain a beacon for their theological descendants. Yet these descendants are still largely isolated, still relatively unconcerned about the wider American scene and only just beginning to exert an influence in that larger arena.

The Princeton Theology, by contrast, proved both consistent and influential. Of major American seminaries besides Princeton, only the Harvard Divinity School could claim that its teaching remained relatively stable over the first century of its existence. But unlike Princeton, the Harvard Divinity School was not a national force. The Calvinism of Princeton, on the other hand, was remarkably powerful for more than a century from 1812 on. This is a major achievement when viewed as a chapter in Reformed history, not for the trivial reason that lack of change somehow implies virtue, but for the much more important reason that the undeviating Princeton convictions were largely Reformed. Everything in the nineteenth century conspired against Calvinist views of humanity and of divine sovereignty. In holding to these positions, the Princeton theologians may have uncritically imbibed a good bit of the American self-determination, especially on matters epistemological, that they professed to repudiate. They may have responded woodenly to a changing philosophical situation. Nonetheless, the constancy of the Princetonians in steadily proclaiming the weakness of human nature and the divinely originated path of salvation, not to speak of their success at shaping institutions to embody this message, testifies to a Reformed vigor the like of which has never been seen in America.

Perhaps it is sufficient to conclude this comparison by saying that Edwards, the Dutch, and Old Princeton each faced cultural-theological crises of considerable magnitude, that each chose somewhat different ways of responding, and that these choices lent each school its distinctive character. Edwards chose to give himself unstintingly to intellectual toil of the most fundamental sort. As a result he left few genuine successors, for those who followed in Edwards's train lacked his powers of insight and his unreserved dependence upon a sovereign God. His books, which have remained to inspire a theologically promiscuous host, constituted his enduring legacy. The Dutch chose the path of cultural formation on a European model. The result was great internal strength, but only slight impact in America at large. Princetonians chose to pour their energies into a seminary devoted to dogmatic inquiry. The result was considerable ambiguity in relationship to American thought and social conditions, but also extraordinary influence within the American milieu.

The Princeton Theology Today

The steady reprinting of books from Old Princeton as well as a continuing, if not overwhelming, flow of critical attention testifies to the vitality of this school among Reformed and evangelical Americans at the end of the twentieth century. Nonetheless, it is no revelation to say that the unique blend of concerns and institutions that constituted the Princeton Theology has passed away. A brief survey of the conservative Reformed denominations, where one might naturally expect to find a continuing Princeton Theology, testifies instead to its absence. Within the Orthodox Presbyterian Church and at Westminster Theological Seminary, great respect remains for the Princeton Theology, but the presuppositional apologetics of Cornelius Van Til has largely replaced Old Princeton's commitment to the Scottish Philosophy of Common Sense, and so unhinged one of its crucial elements. In the Christian Reformed Church, which lacked organic historical connections to Old Princeton to begin with, other varieties of Dutch epistemology—from Kuyper, Bavinck, or Dooyeweerd—take the place of Princeton beliefs about apologetics and religious knowledge. Theologians in the Presbyterian Church of America (PCA) speak kindly of Old Princeton, but here again, philosophical, apologetic, or intellectual tendencies exist that distance members of this body from the Princetonians. The ecclesiology of Thornwell and Dabney, the prospects of Christian Reconstruction, or even a spirit disinclined to sophisticated academic endeavor provide alternative theological foundations in the PCA to those that Old Princeton affirmed. Only a scattering of individuals today combine Augustinian Calvinism, empirical realism, evidentialist apologetics, and piety based on propositions in the manner of the Princeton theologians.

This is not to say that individual parts of their theology do not remain influential. The historical work of Ernest Sandeen, as well as the ongoing efforts of the International Council on Biblical Inerrancy, shows how important the Princeton views on Scripture, especially as refined by Warfield, still are.[42] In addition, the apologetic strategies of the school enjoy considerable currency; some evidentialists who emphasize the reliability of consciousness, logic, and history in demonstrating the truthfulness of the faith make their debt to Old Princeton explicit.[43]

In all this, however, a historian may be pardoned for wondering if the burden of the Princetonians, the critical position that made them a great force for the faith in the nineteenth century, has not been overlooked in our day. Helpful or harmful as their particular views on inspiration and apologetics may be, the Princeton theologians looked upon these matters as subordinate constituents of a more general theology whose end was to glorify God in his greatness and rejoice in the mercies of his salvation. As with so many things in our century, the tendency is to concentrate on means and slight the end. During the nineteenth century the Princeton Theology stood for divine grace, it stood against human pretense in self-salvation and self-revelation, it proclaimed the moral weakness of humanity, and it championed a salvation won for us by God himself. These are the themes that the latter-day friends of the Princeton Theology too often neglect and its latter-day critics too often avoid. But these are also the themes that, if they could be revived, might constitute the greatest gift of Old Princeton to the contemporary world.

During his great debate with E. A. Park in 1850 over the intellectual apprehension of Christianity and the role of the feelings, Charles Hodge paused to summarize the foundation stones of his faith, for which he was prepared to battle without ceasing: "That a sentence of condemnation passed on all men for the sin of one man; that men are by nature the children of wrath; that without Christ we can do nothing; that he hath redeemed us from the curse of the law by being made a curse for us; that men are not merely pardoned but justified." Hodge continued that, by dividing the mind and the heart, Park was preparing "a weapon" against these beliefs. He then closed with a word of hope that Hodge applied to the doctrines themselves but that an admirer can apply to the Princeton version of these convictions as well: "Our consolation is that however keen may be the edge or bright the polish of that weapon, it has so little substance, it must be shivered into atoms with the first blow it strikes against those sturdy trees which have stood for ages in the garden of the Lord and whose leaves have been for the healing of the nations."[44]

Notes: The Princeton Theology

1. Some of the themes developed in this essay are similar to those that introduce the anthology *The Princeton Theology 1812-1921: Scripture, Science, and*

Theological Method from Archibald Alexander to Benjamin Warfield, ed. Mark A. Noll (Grand Rapids: Baker Book House, 1983). This anthology also contains a detailed bibliography and fuller notes than are possible here.

2. See James Waddel Alexander, *The Life of Archibald Alexander* (New York: Charles Scribner's Sons, 1854); and Lefferts A. Loetscher, *Facing the Enlightenment and Pietism: Archibald Alexander and the Founding of Princeton Theological Seminary* (Westport, CT: Greenwood Press, 1983).

3. The basic biography for Charles Hodge is the life by his son, A. A. Hodge, published by Charles Scribner's Sons in 1880. In the absence of a good biography for Warfield, John E. Meeter and Roger Nicole, *A Bibliography of Benjamin Breckinridge Warfield 1851-1921* (Nutley, NJ: Presbyterian and Reformed Publishing Company, 1974), is invaluable.

4. On these individuals, see *The Princeton Theology 1812-1921,* 14-16.

5. Francis Landy Patton, "Princeton Seminary and the Faith," in *The Centennial Celebration of the Theological Seminary of the Presbyterian Church in the United States of America at Princeton, New Jersey* (Princeton: Princeton Theological Seminary, 1910), 349-50. Frank Hugh Foster, *A Genetic History of the New England Theology* (Chicago: University of Chicago Press, 1907), 432.

6. B. B. Warfield, "What is Calvinism?" in *Selected Shorter Writings of Benjamin B. Warfield,* ed. John E. Meeter, 2 vols. (Nutley, NJ: Presbyterian and Reformed Publishing Company, 1970, 1973), 1:389.

7. On Turretin's role at Princeton, see *The Princeton Theology 1812-1921,* 28-30, 116. On the Old Princeton understanding of history, see George Marsden, "J. Gresham Machen, History, and Truth," *Westminster Theological Journal* 42 (Fall 1979): 157-75.

8. Archibald Alexander, *The Sermon, Delivered at the Inauguration of the Rev. Archibald Alexander* (New York: J. Seymour, 1812).

9. B. B. Warfield, "Inspiration," in *International Standard Bible Encyclopedia* (Chicago: Howard-Severance, 1915), as reprinted in *The Works of Benjamin B. Warfield,* vol. 1, *Revelation and Inspiration* (Grand Rapids: Baker Book House, 1981), 96.

10. A. A. Hodge and Warfield, *Inspiration,* introduction by Roger R. Nicole (Grand Rapids: Baker Book House, 1979).

11. Hodge, "The Latest Form of Infidelity," *Biblical Repertory and Princeton Review* 12 (January 1840), as reprinted in Hodge's *Essays and Reviews* (New York: Robert Carter & Brothers, 1857), 90.

12. For example, Alexander, *Inaugural Address;* Warfield, review of Herman Bavinck's *De Zekerheid des Geloofs* in *Princeton Theological Review* 1 (January 1903): 138-43, reprinted in *Selected Shorter Writings of Warfield,* 2:117-22.

13. See William S. Barker, "The Social Views of Charles Hodge: A Study in 19th-Century Calvinism and Conservatism," *Presbyterian: Covenant Seminary Review* 1 (Spring 1975): 1-22.

14. A good discussion of these different approaches is Richard J. Mouw, "The Bible in Twentieth-Century Protestantism: A Preliminary Taxonomy," in *The Bible in America: Essays in Cultural History,* eds. Nathan O. Hatch and Mark A. Noll (New York: Oxford University Press, 1982), 139-62, with 143-44 on the doctrinal emphases of Old Princeton.

15. See, in general, James R. Moore, *The Post-Darwinian Controversies: A Study of the Protestant Struggle to Come to Terms with Darwin in Great Britain and America, 1870-1900* (Cambridge: Cambridge University Press, 1979); and, more specifically, David N. Livingstone, "The Idea of Design: The Vicissitudes of a

Key Concept in the Princeton Response to Darwin," *Scottish Journal of Theology* 37 (1984): 329-57.

16. Sydney E. Ahlstrom, "The Scottish Philosophy and American Theology," *Church History* 24 (1955): 257-72. An early work commenting on Princeton's use of the Scottish Philosophy was Ralph J. Danhof, *Charles Hodge as Dogmatician* (Goes, The Netherlands: Oosterbaan and le Cointre, 1929). The fullest consideration of this subject is now John C. Vander Stelt, *Philosophy and Scripture: A Study in Old Princeton and Westminster Theology* (Marlton, NJ: Mack Publishing Company, 1978).

17. See Wesley Frank Craven, "William Graham," in *Princetonians 1769-1775: A Biographical Dictionary*, ed. Richard A. Harrison (Princeton: Princeton University Press, 1980), 289-94.

18. For an excellent general picture, see Henry F. May, *The Enlightenment in America* (New York: Oxford University Press, 1976).

19. Alexander, "The Nature and Evidence of Truth," in *The Princeton Theology 1812-1921*, 61-71; Alexander, *Outlines of Moral Science* (New York: Charles Scribner's Sons, 1852).

20. The best study of this enthusiasm for the new science among theologians is Theodore Dwight Bozeman, *Protestantism in an Age of Science: The Baconian Ideal and Antebellum American Religious Thought* (Chapel Hill: University of North Carolina Press, 1977).

21. Hodge, *Systematic Theology*, 3 vols. (Grand Rapids: Wm. B. Eerdmans Publishing Company, 1946), 1:10.

22. The different uses of this philosophy by evangelicals is discussed in Mark A. Noll, "Common Sense Traditions and American Evangelical Thought," *American Quarterly* 37 (Summer 1985): 216-38.

23. Park, "New England Theology," *Bibliotheca Sacra* 9 (January 1852): 191-92.

24. For comparison, see, on the power of the New England Theology, Bruce Kuklick, *Churchmen and Philosophers: From Jonathan Edwards to John Dewey* (New Haven: Yale University Press, 1985); and on Bushnell, Daniel Walker Howe, "The Social Science of Horace Bushnell," *Journal of American History* 70 (September 1983): 305-22.

25. See especially the discussion of Alexander's ethics in D. H. Meyer, *The Instructed Conscience: The Shaping of the American National Ethic* (Philadelphia: University of Pennsylvania Press, 1972), 55-58.

26. On the more general trends, see Nathan O. Hatch, "The Christian Movement and the Demand for a Theology of the People," *Journal of American History* 67 (December 1980): 545-67; and Hatch, "Evangelicalism as a Democratic Movement," in *Evangelicalism and Modern America*, ed. George M. Marsden (Grand Rapids: Wm. B. Eerdmans Publishing Company, 1984).

27. A thorough recent discussion of these emphases is Steven L. Martin, "The Doctrines of Man, Reason and the Holy Spirit in the Epistemology of Charles Hodge" (M.A. Thesis, Trinity Evangelical Divinity School, 1984).

28. Warfield's discussions of the human elements in biblical inspiration and of natural processes in the creation of the natural world illustrate the sophistication of this useful theological construction. See *The Princeton Theology 1812-1921*, 268-79, 293-98.

29. Hoffecker, *Piety and the Princetonians: Archibald Alexander, Charles Hodge, and Benjamin Warfield* (Phillipsburg, NJ: Presbyterian and Reformed Publishing Company, 1981).

30. Kelsey, *The Uses of Scripture in Recent Theology* (Philadelphia: Fortress Press, 1975), 17-24.

31. See Mark A. Noll, "The Founding of Princeton Seminary," *Westminster Theological Journal* 42 (Fall 1979): 72-110; and *The Princeton Theology 1812-1921*, 18-20, 51-58.

32. See *The Princeton Theology 1812-1921*, 22-24, for a discussion of the various Princeton journals from 1825 to 1929.

33. To obtain an overview of the work of this journal, see *Biblical Repertory and Princeton Review. Index Volume from 1825 to 1868*, 3 vols. (Philadelphia: Peter Walker, 1870-71).

34. Charles Hodge, "The *Princeton Review* on the State of the Country and of the Church," *Biblical Repertory and Princeton Review* 37 (October 1865): 687.

35. Cited in A. A. Hodge, *Life of Charles Hodge*, 257, 259-60.

36. A good modern treatment of Old Princeton positions is to be found, emphasis of the title notwithstanding, in George M. Marsden, *The Evangelical Mind and the New School Presbyterian Experience* (New Haven: Yale University Press, 1970).

37. *Biblical Repertory and Princeton Review. Index Volume*, 2:206.

38. See Noll, "Common Sense Traditions and American Evangelical Thought," *American Quarterly*.

39. Randall H. Balmer, "The Princetonians and Scripture: A Reconsideration," *Westminster Theological Journal* 44 (1982): 352-65; Balmer and John D. Woodbridge, "The Princetonians' Viewpoint of Biblical Authority: An Evaluation of Ernest Sandeen," in *Scripture and Truth*, eds. Woodbridge and D. A. Carson (Grand Rapids: Zondervan Publishing House, 1983). Woodbridge and Balmer rightly criticize Sandeen for suggesting that Old Princeton invented the concept of biblical inerrancy (see Sandeen, *The Roots of Fundamentalism: British and American Millenarianism 1800-1930* [Chicago: University of Chicago Press, 1970]; and "The Princeton Theology: One Source of Biblical Literalism in American Protestantism," *Church History* 31 [September 1962]: 307-21). Still, a modified version of Sandeen's argument—that Princeton refined, clarified, and emphasized certain aspects of the common evangelical heritage concerning Scripture—is quite defensible. Sandeen's work on fundamentalism, as well as other standard treatments of the subject that document the eager fundamentalist use of Princeton's views on Scripture (e.g., George W. Dollar, *A History of Fundamentalism in America* [Greenville, SC: Bob Jones University Press, 1973]; George M. Marsden, *Fundamentalism and American Culture* [New York: Oxford University Press, 1980]), suggests two things: (1) that fundamentalists recognized the Princeton formulation as a powerful statement of their sometimes inarticulate convictions, but also (2) that A. A. Hodge and Warfield were in fact highlighting in a new, effective way elements of an earlier, more amorphous confidence in Scripture.

40. On this widespread trust in a simple scientific epistemology, see, among many others, Bozeman, *Protestants in an Age of Science*; Henry Warner Bowden, *Church History in the Age of Science: Historiographical Patterns in the United States 1876-1918* (Chapel Hill: University of North Carolina Press, 1971); Foster, *New England Theology*; E. Brooks Holifield, *The Gentlemen Theologians: American Theology in Southern Culture, 1795-1860* (Durham, NC: Duke University Press, 1978); Herbert Hovenkamp, *Science and Religion in America, 1800-1860* (Philadelphia: University of Pennsylvania Press, 1978); Daniel Walker Howe, *The Unitarian Conscience: Harvard Moral Philosophy, 1805-1861* (Cambridge: Harvard University Press, 1970); May, *The Enlightenment in America*; Meyer, *The Instructed Conscience*;

Alexandra Oleson and Sanborn C. Brown, eds., *The Pursuit of Knowledge in the Early American Republic: American Scientific and Learned Societies from Colonial Times to the Civil War* (Baltimore: Johns Hopkins University Press, 1976); Douglas Sloan, *The Scottish Enlightenment and the American College Ideal* (New York: Teachers College Press, 1961); and Laurence R. Veysey, *The Emergence of the American University* (Chicago: University of Chicago Press, 1965).

41. The best work I have seen in comparing Princeton and the Dutch is by Stephen R. Spencer of Grand Rapids Baptist Seminary, "A Comparison and Evaluation of the Old Princeton and Amsterdam Apologetics" (Th.M. Thesis, Grand Rapids Baptist Seminary, n.d.). On connections between Edwards and the Princetonians, see Mark A. Noll, "Jonathan Edwards and Nineteenth-Century Theology," in *Jonathan Edwards and the American Experience*, eds. Nathan O. Hatch and Harry S. Stout (forthcoming); and on relations between Warfield and Kuyper and Bavinck, *The Princeton Theology 1812-1921*, 302-07.

42. Sandeen, *The Roots of Fundamentalism*; at least two recent books by the Inerrancy Council feature consideration of Old Princeton: see John Gerstner, "The Contributions of Charles Hodge, B. B. Warfield, and J. Gresham Machen to the Doctrine of Inspiration," in *Challenges to Inerrancy: A Theological Response*, eds. Gordon R. Lewis and Bruce Demarest (Chicago: Moody Press, 1984); and D. Clair Davis, "Princeton and Inerrancy: The Nineteenth-Century Theological Background of Contemporary Concerns," in *Inerrancy and the Church*, ed. John D. Hannah (Chicago: Moody Press, 1984).

43. For example, R. C. Sproul, John Gerstner, and Arthur Lindsley, *Classical Apologetics: A Rational Defense of the Christian Faith and a Critique of Presuppositional Apologetics* (Grand Rapids: Zondervan Publishing House, 1984).

44. Hodge, "The Theology of the Intellect and That of the Feelings," *Biblical Repertory and Princeton Review* 22 (October 1850): 674; reprinted in *Essays and Reviews*, 569.

2

CHARLES HODGE

DAVID F. WELLS

Charles Hodge

THE mainstay of Protestant orthodoxy in the nineteenth century, both within Presbyterianism and the wider evangelical movement, was Princeton Theological Seminary. And Princeton, during most of these years, was identified substantially with the work of its most formidable representative, Charles Hodge. Hodge taught there from 1822, ten years after the founding of the Seminary, almost to his death in 1878, except for two years of study abroad in Germany. The celebration of the fiftieth year of his professorship in 1872 was without precedent in American academic life. Even the shops in Princeton closed on this day to honor a patriarch, a theologian, and a teacher of more than three thousand ministerial students.[1]

Hodge's theological views were formed remarkably early, and in the long and unremitting struggle with the New School thinkers, a struggle that occupied him for much of his life, he defended his convictions unflinchingly and unswervingly. It is true that his *Systematic Theology*, written late in his life as a replacement for the Latin text that had been used at Princeton—Turretin's *Institutio theologiae elencticae*—does evidence a mellower tone than his essays published earlier in *The Biblical Repertory and Princeton Review*, but changes in his theology were few and far between. It was the stout consistency of Hodge's theology and the rigorous defense he gave of it that earned him an almost oracular standing among Old Schoolers. And, with the passing of the years, it created an identity between Hodge's outlook and that of the Seminary. "Princeton theology" in the early years was really Charles Hodge's theology.

Posterity, however, has not always dealt kindly with Hodge, and certainly the perspective in which we now view his theological accomplishments is quite different from that in which his contemporaries viewed them. This is particularly evident at three points. First, we usually identify Hodge's theology with his three-volume *Systematic Theol-*

ogy; his contemporaries for the most part did not. They knew him principally as an essayist and polemicist. Long before the thick volumes of his *Systematic* appeared in 1872 and 1873, he had forged his place in American church life with his incisive and rigorous excursions in the *Biblical Repertory* and its successors. There is a passion and liveliness in these essays that is sometimes absent from his systematic theology.

Second, the cultural and ecclesiastical context in which Hodge was writing has today largely been forgotten. In part, of course, Hodge is himself responsible for this. The fact that he was living in a time of dramatic social and intellectual change within the country is not always evident in the pages of his *Theology;* indeed, he often ignored the world around him much as Jane Austen's novels did the Napoleonic Wars. Yet it is this context that actually engaged Hodge all of his life. He and his colleagues at Princeton worked within the lengthening shadow of the country's "infidelity," against those who were perceived to have been tainted by it theologically, and alongside those through whom revival was occurring but whose means and methods were creating ecclesiastical chaos. Hodge cannot be understood adequately if he is divorced from this context and yet, paradoxically, his *Systematic Theology* gives us insufficient help in understanding it.

Third, the argument that biblical inerrancy was a Princetonian creation has resulted in an obsessive interest in the formulation of this tenet and it has skewered our assessment of Hodge. A contemporary of Hodge would have noticed that while he affirmed his belief in the integrity of Scripture, he spent relatively little time formulating and defending it. Hodge's theological interests lay elsewhere. They were interests foisted upon him by his religious and cultural context. The hotly contested issues, the questions that called forth his great polemical powers, were, as Earl Kennedy has noted, "the doctrines of the imputation of Adam's sin, original sin, inability, and regeneration."[2] These were the issues on which Hodge forged a distinctive position as he stated his opposition to New Schoolers like Nathaniel William Taylor, revivalists like Charles Finney, the "progressive orthodox" like Horace Bushnell, the Unitarians, and, beyond them, a culture turned self-confident in its post-Enlightenment rationalism.

It is this obscured Hodge, the forgotten Hodge, the polemical Hodge, upon which this essay is focused, not the Hodge of later years who is reflected—and, some say buried—in the stout volumes of his *Systematic Theology*. First, then, I want to develop the Princetonians' perceptions of the religious state of the country and consider some of the consequences of these perceptions. Second, I will elaborate upon the contest between the Old School and New School theologies but especially as this was focused in the contest between the faculties at Yale and Princeton.

Third, I want to examine Hodge's view of the atonement, which, with its closely related issues, was at the center of his debate with Nathaniel Taylor of Yale.

Declension and Infidelity

At the beginning of the nineteenth century much of American Christianity was at the nadir of its fortunes. This, at least, was the view of many of the influential orthodox clergymen. The 1730s and 1740s, when the whole eastern seaboard had glowed with the incandescent light of the Great Awakening, were followed, as they saw it, by five decades of lethargy and declension. In these years, the Church was graced with few great divines and even fewer reports of revival. The scenes of uproar, repentance, transformation, and exultation that had marked the days of Edwards and Whitefield were not repeated; they passed into the faded corridors of Christian memory where they quietly expired.

At the same time, Enlightenment ideas were flooding into the country. Colonial militia found themselves in the company of British and French troops whose Christian views were at best uncertain and whose morals were invariably loose. The Revolution opened the door still wider to various forms of rationalism, for the French, many of whom according to Timothy Dwight were possessed "of ardent minds and daring speculations," sided with the aggrieved colonists. "No knight errant ever offered himself to an affrighted damsel with more generosity as her protector," Dwight complained, "than they to the human race."[3] The Revolution, he claimed, brought with it "a long train of immoral doctrines and practices which spread into every corner of the country."[4]

This became the common perception among ministers at the turn of the century and provided the impetus for many a sermonic foray on a Sunday morning. In a typical analysis, Joseph Lathrop reminded his congregation in 1798 that:

> In these American States, there has, for many years, and more especially since our late revolution, been a visible tendency to infidelity, and an observable growth in impiety and immorality. Family religion is falling into disuse; the ancient strict observance of the Sabbath is mightily relaxed, social worship in the church, as well as in the family, is sinking into neglect, not to say contempt. . . . In this state of general indifference, the barriers against infidelity are fallen down, and the way is open for its swift and easy progress.[5]

Lathrop went on to speak of how swiftly and easily infidelity was actually progressing. Licentious books were multiplying and circulating "without modesty," even finding their way into the stacks of "social libraries." Other people, trafficking in "indecent ridicule and malignant satire," had attacked the Bible itself. Ministers spoke of the corruption of justice that had resulted, of the growth of taverns and of tippling, of sabbath desecration, of the abuse of children, and of riots and licentiousness.[6]

The alarm thus sounded, the faithful rose as one to defend the land against further intrusion of infidelity. But what was quickly discovered was that there was no single enemy. Infidelity was a synonym for the whole range of departures from Christian faith, be they small or large.

The most flagrant expression of infidelity was found among the devotees of irreligion who followed in Thomas Paine's footsteps, although they never posed a serious challenge to more orthodox faith. In 1825 the Free Press Association was formed with its literary outlet, *The Correspondent*. A freethinkers' society that deliberately profaned the sabbath by sponsoring lectures on that day sprang up in New York. By 1830 it was rumored that twenty thousand people had been attracted to these lectures. Although this figure appears to be an exaggeration, it is undoubtedly true that anti-Christian sentiment was gaining popular support. Similar societies began to appear in other cities. In 1831 Boston saw the creation of the First Society of Free Thinkers, which was dedicated to the pursuit of "useful knowledge" such as the education of children "without regard to religious opinions." In 1835 these and other societies were linked together in a national network through the creation of the United States Moral and Philosophical Society.

The specter of unbelief, organizing itself, capitalizing on the economic disorders to enlist support for its socialism, and breeding communes and subversive ideas, greatly alarmed Christian leaders, who exaggerated its importance. Horace Bushnell, who did not panic easily, wrote in 1835 of the "considerable number" of societies of freethinkers, which were growing with "fearful rapidity." He thought he discerned why the movement was gaining ground. By opposing religion, private property, and marriage, he asserted, "they unite irreligion, rapacity and lust."[7] Therein lay their power. However, just as the movement began to gather momentum it began to disintegrate from within. By the early 1840s it had expired, the victim of apathy, inertia, penury, a bad reputation, and the devastation of the Second Great Awakening. Those who might have lent a hand to freethinking now called themselves "liberals" and abandoned the movement to its own failing devices.

The transition from "liberalism" to Unitarianism took place between 1805 and 1819. In 1805 Henry Ware was elected to the Hollis chair of theology at Harvard. In reaction to this appointment, Andover Theological Seminary was founded in 1807 to preserve and defend Christian orthodoxy, its two most distinguished faculty recruits being Moses Stuart and Leonard Woods. Orthodoxy and Christian "infidelity" were thus becoming entrenched on opposing sides of the battle.

The controversy with the emerging Unitarianism was sparked in 1815. A book inspired by Jedediah Morse was published and reviewed by the orthodox journal, *Panoplist*.[8] This drew a response from William Channing, the Unitarian luminary, that was answered by Noah Worcester. Channing then wrote two additional letters and Worcester wrote three.[9] In 1819, the controversy was suspended, but not before the orthodox had achieved their aim. "Unitarianism," observed Wisner, "which had before operated and spread in secret, was brought to light."[10] The entire subject was illumined still further by Channing himself in that same year, 1819, when in the course of an ordination sermon he systematically defended Unitarianism.[11] For the first time, responded Taylor, the world was informed about what Unitarians *did* believe rather than what they *did not* believe! Instead of "sneers and insinuations," the orthodox had some solid arguments to oppose. And oppose them they did. Channing's defense precipitated several rather complex literary duels between himself and Stuart, between Leonard Woods and Henry Ware,[12] and, in 1821, between Samuel Miller, Charles Hodge's colleague at Princeton, and the Unitarian movement as a whole.[13]

From 1821 to 1827 the New School Connecticut Calvinists spearheaded the assault on this, the latest form of Bostonian liberalism, but two new elements were added to the controversy. First, the battle was taken to Boston itself by Lyman Beecher. The object was to deprive Unitarianism of its popular support by bringing the city under the sound of revival preaching. Second, Nathaniel Taylor, professor of theology at Yale, who was most dissatisfied with the approach of the Andover theologians and offered the opinion that they had set the cause of orthodoxy back by fifty years, developed a new apologetic by softening the doctrine of human depravity, which was the most important bone of contention. Taylor was also changing direction, it needs to be noted, because he accepted the estimate made of human nature by the Scottish Common Sense realism.

Beecher's responsibility in checking Unitarianism was to advance to Boston with the Christian gospel, but when he arrived he came as a man of peace; he had honey on his tongue. Not one "knocking down" sermon was preached, he informed a friend. "I have not felt *once* the spirit of rebuke; have not uttered an ironical or sarcastic expression; have not struck one stroke at an antagonist."[14] What was needed, he said, was "luminous exposition" that wooed rather than battered, because ordinary Unitarians were not so much opposed to Christian orthodoxy as ignorant of it. They had never really had a chance to reject it. The strategy was most effective. "New cases of inquiry and of hope appear every week," he wrote, "and an impression is made among the Unitarian population too deep and solemn in favor of the revival to allow their ministers to preach against it."[15] A little less irenically, he later exulted that "orthodoxy in Massachusetts is becoming a phalanx terrible as an army with banners, and that our adversaries shall no more be able to frame iniquity by law, and draw sin as with a cart-rope."[16] Thus were his opponents left to splutter feebly as their congregations were wooed away and the ground was cut from beneath their feet. Here was Beecher, by his own admission "a man of war" from his youth upward, melting impenitent infidels with his soft words while from afar his friend, Nathaniel Taylor, was drawing their blood with his sharp treatises. It is an arresting picture.

This context deeply affected the form and direction that Hodge's theology took. First, the debate with Unitarianism, in which the Princetonians also participated, set up a deep cleavage between the New School and Old School divines. New Schoolers like Beecher and Taylor were embarrassed by the defense of Old School Calvinism made by Hodge, Woods, and Stuart. Hodge, in turn, was scandalized by the defense offered by Taylor. What the Yale divine was advocating seemed to be indistinguishable from Pelagianism. Thus were the battle lines drawn within Presbyterian and Congregational circles.

Second, the alarming situation in the country awakened the Princetonians to the need for a defense of Christianity as a whole. This was present incipiently in Hodge, although it was not to come into full bloom until a little later when Francis Patton and B. B. Warfield began their work. The emergence of apologetics as a fundamental and central concern, not merely as a peripheral exercise, was a nineteenth-century interest; more precisely, it was Princeton's innovation. It was born in a deep commitment to defend biblical faith in all of its essentials. It was this commitment that really explains Charles Hodge.

The New Theology and the Old

A reviewer of E. A. Park's *The Atonement*, a volume of considerable importance for New England theology, declared optimistically in 1854 that "there is general agreement in these views by Evangelical Christians—certainly here in New England."[17] There was, as a matter of fact, general agreement on Park's collected essays neither in New England nor anywhere else. A century earlier, there had been unanimity but for those of a more traditional bent all of this had changed when Taylor had been appointed at Yale and, according to Ebenezer Porter of Andover, had volunteered to shed darkness on the world. It was not long before the "old paths began to be called in question," another dissatisfied author said, "and the ardor of youth began to be enlisted in making new discoveries in the polar regions of speculation," especially, he noted, with respect to finding "a channel of communication between Calvinism and Pelagianism."[18] Likewise an anonymous Presbyterian speaking for the Old School charged that the New Haven divines, philosophizing to faith rather than from faith and trafficking in Scholasticism's "subtle questions," "endless logomachies," and "absurd barbarisms," had unfortunately drifted into "Arminian, Socinian, Arian and Pelagian errors."[19] This was a new turn of events, for as late as 1755 President Clap had claimed that all tutors at Yale were, as a matter of course, examined theologically and, if found guilty of Arminian or "Prelatical principles," were summarily suspended. The "New Scheme of Divinity," which Clap himself had assembled from various New England divines, was not, to judge from Hodge's review of Clap,[20] altogether above suspicion, but certainly Taylor had taken prevailing tendencies to an extreme. And when the Yale divine made his coy retreats into doubt—"it may be no one can prove" or "how do you know?"—it seemed to many Old Schoolers that he was using phrases that, "like a magic wand, have made truth and error appear alike."[21] Consequently, Charles Hodge argued that the bearers of the authentic Edwardsean mantle were the Princetonians, despite the fact that Edwards's Idealism made them a little nervous. The tradition of Dwight, Emmons, and Hopkins was being substantially preserved at Princeton and substantially subverted at Yale.

Hodge took the long view as to why this conflict had arisen. He argued that from its inception Christianity had been plagued by the conflict between two competing doctrinal systems. The one, he said, "has for its object the vindication of the Divine supremacy and sovereignty in the salvation of men; the other has for its characteristic aim the assertion of the rights of human nature. It is specially solicitous that nothing should be held to be true, which cannot be philosophically reconciled with the liberty and ability of man."[22] These competing outlooks, Hodge believed, were again at war in the nineteenth century, each claiming to be the true representative of biblical faith and both asking for the allegiance of the church. Subsequently, of course, historians have come to see that there were many other factors involved in this growing bifurcation, yet it is undeniable that at its center was a contest between two types of Reformed theology and two different estimates of the degree and consequences of human corruption.

In 1820 Taylor judged that the moment was ripe to attack the Unitarians. His objective, however, was only partly that of exposing them for the infidels he judged them to be; his other aim was to hoist to the flagpole of orthodoxy a different kind of Calvinism from the one that the Unitarians had so confidently been mocking.

The point at which Taylor entered the fray was after the ground had been cleared by the debate between Woods of Andover and Henry Ware of Harvard. Taylor now took on another Harvard divine, Andrews Norton.[23] What Taylor sought to show was that the opponents of Calvinism "never fairly attack its doctrines, as they are stated by Calvin himself, or exhibited in the creeds of the churches, or in the writings of the authors which bear his name";[24] these opponents attacked straw men! Specifically, they held up to ridicule a doctrine of human nature that even the sects would consider to be injurious and false. Calvinists in fact believed, said Taylor, that "mankind come [sic] into the world in such a state, that without the interposition of divine grace, all as soon as they became moral agents, sin in every accountable act."[25] This belief in depravity, he said, must be distinguished from "theories" about it. Among these theories was the notion of "the imputation of Adam's sin to his posterity."[26] Sin is not imputed; at least, it is not imputed in the way that Old Schoolers like Hodge imagined. All are born with a corrupted nature, Taylor affirmed, but this is not in and of itself sinful. This corrupted nature only provides the occasion for our sinning when the agent is of a morally accountable age. Furthermore, people sin inevitably, said Taylor, but not necessarily. This was a subtle distinction that the Yale professor would be called upon to defend more than once in the ensuing controversy. But it allowed Taylor to argue that his Calvinism, which he believed to be historic Calvinism, differed from that espoused at Princeton.

Posing the issue in this way appeared to Beecher to be a stroke of brilliance, and it is undeniable that it did relieve the Connecticut Calvinists of some hard apologetic tasks. Unitarians, for example, had been able to expose the harshness of Calvinistic doctrine by picturing hell as paved with the remains of innocent babies.[27] This could now be denied *fortissimo*. To Beecher Nettleton wrote: "I believe it to be a matter of fact that you and I are *really* a different kind of Calvinist from what the Unitarians have imagined or been accustomed to imagine."[28] He suggested that the New Haveners should argue that they had no interest in defending "old Calvinism"; their sole concern was with the "evangelical system." Beecher apparently accepted this as sound advice. Late in 1829, he went up to Boston to deliver a series of discourses on political atheism. On that subject, as he said, he "opened the ground tier; and let out, without let or hindrance, all the caustics in the locker."[29] He also let out a few caustics on "old Calvinism." Referring to the old view of Adam's solidarity with the human race and the imputation of his sin to all people, he said: "It is my deliberate opinion that the false philosophy which has been employed for the exposition of the Calvinistic system has done more to obstruct the march of Christianity, and to paralyze the saving power of the Gospel . . . than all other causes beside."[30] By an unnatural collusion, the Connecticut Calvinists seemed to be uniting in part with the Unitarians against the more traditional Calvinists like Hodge. This was a maneuver fraught with danger, as they were soon to discover. For while the emancipation from "old Calvinism" might be used to discomfort Unitarians by denying them their best arguments, it could also be used against those Calvinists who were thus emancipated. Unitarians seemed to grasp that the sword had two edges far more rapidly than did Taylor and his friends.

Initially, the new twist that Taylor was trying to put into Calvinism was hailed by the Unitarians as a sign that Taylor was in full flight. Realizing that "old Calvinism" was indefensible, Taylor had moved on to new ground. Then the full implication of what was taking place seemed to dawn on them even more fully. In the same year that Taylor was concluding his debate with Norton, the *Christian Examiner* decided to review a sermon of Beecher's. The reviewer spoke of "its decidedly *anti-*Calvinistic leaning." What he meant, the reviewer went on to say, was that Beecher had denied some of the "peculiarities" of Calvinism and had distinctly asserted none of them. As to particulars, the author argued that Beecher had asserted "in as strong and unqualified language as was ever used by an Arminian or Unitarian, the doctrine of man's actual *ability* and *free agency*. . . . On the doctrine of *original sin* and *native depravity*, our author is hardly less unsound in his orthodoxy." Even the doctrine of atonement, he added, "might also be adopted by all Unitarians of whom we have any knowledge."[31]

The new apologetic must have appeared almost heaven sent to the Unitarians and they were quick to exploit it. Yale was played off against Andover, then against Princeton. In the meantime, Taylor's own Calvinism had clarified further in the new direction. The 1828 *Concio ad Clerum* that he delivered to the Congregational clergy of Connecticut was a manifesto for, even an explication of, the new position. With flamboyance and subtlety, he spelled out in some detail what Calvinism meant vis-à-vis the issues raised in the debates. The Unitarians hailed the address as "able and satisfactory." They saw sure signs everywhere that Calvinists were "silently but surely advancing towards the very opinions they so eagerly condemn."[32] More embarrassing accolades could not have been heard. Disquieted and anxious about Taylor's views, many Calvinists began to have second thoughts about New Haven theology. In the following year, 1829, the Unitarians were given a break that was not altogether unexpected. The orthodox divided against themselves.

Taylor's address, *Concio ad Clerum*, had served as a call to arms for the Princetonians. Alexander fired off a broadside against Pelagianism. This was followed by a heated exchange between Hodge and Goodrich, who had earlier purchased *The Quarterly Christian Spectator* as a literary outlet for the Yale divines and as a voice for the New Theology. The debate was over what, from a historical point of view, constitutes historic Calvinism. Goodrich was simply taking Taylor's defense against the Unitarians and turning it into an aggressive offense against the Princetonians. In this he was modestly successful, for he was able to show that Hodge was not as competent historically as he was in other ways. Hodge had participated in an evolution within Calvinism without being fully aware of the reasons for or results of that change. Goodrich's success, however, had only a little to do with the theological issues at stake, and on these matters Hodge was unmovable.

The inevitable parting of the ways came in 1837. In that year, the General Assembly, at the instigation of the Princetonians, and especially of Hodge, abrogated the Plan of Union of 1801, thereby excising approximately sixty thousand church members and ministers from four synods, most of whom were predominantly under New School influence.[33] Sympathizers of the New Schoolers like Leonard Bacon expressed their outrage, complaining that "their titles to all their church property [were] put at hazard without the form of a trial, without the citation of a witness, without the opportunity of defence, after having been reproached in mass, as disorganizers and heretics, and after measures had been commenced leading to a judicial investigation of the charges preferred against them."[34]

Technically, this was correct. Nevertheless, it needs to be remembered that the grounds for the excision were largely theological and these theological issues had been extensively debated in the church during the two decades that preceded this event. It is doubtful whether further debate in 1837 would have provided new light or changed very many opinions. In a roundabout way this was conceded by the New Schoolers who were Congregationalists. They decided in 1852 that Congregationalism should go its own way without any further alliances with the Presbyterians, a preponderance of whom were Old Schoolers. It is this context, of painful theological debate and wrenching ecclesiastical schism, which must be allowed to form the backdrop for Hodge's theological life.

Polemics and Convictions

In the first half of the nineteenth century, down the eastern seaboard at least, ecclesiastical life was much affected by the Second Awakening. What dominated discussion, consequently, were the practical issues that evangelists had to confront. How should conversion be presented? What is a legitimate use of persuasion? What about the Anxious Bench? Can all accept the gospel? Should it be offered indiscriminately to all? These were, of course, the questions provoked in particular by Charles Finney and his "New Measures," and the answers Finney developed had an uncanny resemblance to many of the things that Taylor had been elucidating at Yale.

Hodge was deeply concerned with this development because he saw in its resurgent Pelagianism the supposition that conversion is a merely human work. That being the case, Christ's work on the cross was being emptied of any serious significance. He explained his concern in this way:

> The constant exhortation is, to make choice of God as the portion of the soul, to change the governing purpose of the life, to submit to the moral Governor of the universe the specific act to which the sinner is urged as immediately connected with salvation, is an act which has no reference to Christ. The soul is brought immediately in contact with God, the Mediator is left out of view. We maintain that this is another Gospel. It is practically another system, and a legal system of religion. We do not intend that the doctrine of the mediation of Christ is rejected, but that it is neglected; that the sinner is led to God directly; that he is not urged, under the pressure of the sense of guilt, to go to Christ for pardon, and through him to God, but the general idea of submission (not the specific idea of submission to the plan of salvation through Jesus Christ) is urged as the making a right choice. Conviction of sin is made of little account, Christ and his atonement are kept out of view, so that the matter of salvation is not distinctly presented to the minds of the people.[35]

Hodge saw clearly that soteriological conclusions arise from anthropological premises, that a deficient view of the atonement could not be corrected until the inadequate doctrine of sin had been attacked. It was this that was at the root of the problem and it was this that was attacked with a devotion to principle that was unswerving.

The debate now centered on whether people can be held accountable for what Adam had done. The reverse side of this coin, of course, was whether people could be acquitted by what Christ had done. In each case responsibility was being interpreted corporately, for in each case there was representation of the many by the one. But there were complexities in this that needed to be resolved.[36] In Scripture, condemnation and justification are sentential acts. We are not made unrighteous by being pronounced so any more than we are made holy by being declared justified. We are declared righteous when Christ's righteousness is forensically imputed to us, but does this similarly mean that we are unrighteous only by the judicial reckoning of Adam's sin to us? To allow that this might be so would be to allow a Unitarian conception that we are all natively innocent, that unrighteousness is a matter merely of divine decree and not of human constitution. The idea of condemnation as judicial pronouncement therefore had to be given underpinning in a doctrine of the actual transmission of sin from parent to child. This, however, disturbed the symmetry between the two Adams and their representative roles, for in the one case we are declared righteous without ever actually being so whereas in the other case we are declared unrighteous and we are actually so.

Hodge's solution was forged in direct opposition to the idea of mediate imputation favored by the New School divines. They argued that Adam's posterity was not involved in his sin either because they were in his loins, philosophically speaking (as the Edwardseans believed), or because this sin was simply reckoned to them as the Princetonians said. Imputation, rather, is the transmission of the consequences of that Adamic sin in the legacy of tainted human nature. Sin is, Nathaniel Taylor said, in the sinning. No one sinned in Adam but we do sin because of Adam. We are therefore pronounced guilty when we become culpable for our own sinning and never because we have a connection with Adam's sin. But as this solution was developed both in respect to conversion and in relation to Christ's work, its tendency to become a form of works-salvation, dependent ultimately not on what Christ did and does but upon what we do, became unmistakable. Hodge rejected it unconditionally.

In developing his own view of Adam's federal representation, Hodge was aware that he was taking an unpopular and unfashionable stand. The Old School doctrine, which he only belatedly discovered was not entirely identical with his own, was subjected, he said, to "execration and contempt" from the New School men and a little earlier Alexander had said that they treated it as "so absurd" that they did not condescend to discuss it. This was a provocative statement, for the New School divines were seldom reticent to discuss Old School absurdities!

Hodge dismissed the Idealist's notion of a universal humanity, a generic life common to all people, as "a mere hypothesis,"[37] perhaps not so much out of theological considerations as from philosophical. He was also dissatisfied with the consequent notion of imputation. Edwards's theology used the old word but it had none of the old doctrinal content. But what Edwards had that Nathaniel Taylor lacked was a doctrine of "native depravity"; it was Hodge's agreement with Edwards on this point that he felt entitled him to be called an Edwardsean. It was the deviation from this point by the New Haven theologians that made them usurpers of the Edwardsean heritage. Hodge nevertheless found himself at odds even with the more traditional Edwardseans in explaining how we are culpable for Adam's sin. People have a common nature, Hodge countered, only in the sense that they have a common origin, belong to the same species, have generically identical rational and moral faculties, and are commonly alienated from God at birth. Adam "was an individual man, with no more of the generic life of the race than any other man."[38] Thus Hodge might loudly claim his Edwardsean heritage when in debate with New Haven theologians, but his claim became a good deal more muted when he was in discussion with more conservative followers of Edwards! Indeed, with them Hodge saw his differences with Edwards as more important than his similarities, whereas with Taylor Hodge accentuated his similarities and passed over his differences in silence.

The Protestant Reformers, but in particular John Calvin, included under the single term original sin both the imputed guilt of Adam's sin and the inherent depravity consequent upon it. Hodge believed, however, that it was the latter aspect that the Reformers emphasized. He suggested that this was partly because Roman Catholic theologians at the time held an inadequate view of human corruption and partly because Calvin wanted to affirm that we are not innocent creatures condemned merely because Adam sinned. Hodge himself was to assume Calvin's perspective but only as a result of being embroiled in this extended debate on the subject. Initially he stressed the former aspect, the imputed guilt of Adam's sin, and declared that evangelical religion would survive only if this emphasis was maintained.

The idea of imputation, that one person suffers the penalty for another's sin, he saw to be the working principle of the universe. This principle would still be part of the warp and woof of life even if the Fall, the Bible, and God were to be denied. No man is an island. No one lives out his or her life in a vacuum. The individual acts of one person always touch and affect others. It was the perception of this truth that redeemed Bushnell's study *Christian Nurture*, and it was the failure to see this by the late followers of Edwards that was subverting "the whole evangelical system." For they contended that God could not justly condemn a person for sins other than his or her own. How then, Hodge asked, could he justify a person for righteousness other than that person's own?

The notion of federal representation came into its own when the idea of covenants began to be important.[39] The notion of a probationary period in which the human race was on trial through its representative, Adam, was then advanced. Because of this covenant, only Adam's first sin was imputed to his posterity, for at this point the covenant was abrogated. This was the basis of Hodge's view that, he said, was also stated with "extraordinary unanimity" by both Lutheran and Calvinistic confessions and could be summarized thus:

1. That Adam, as the common father of all men, was by divine appointment constituted not only the natural, but the federal head or representative of his posterity. The race stood its probation in him. His sin was the sin of the race, because the sin of its divinely and righteously constituted representative. We therefore sinned in Adam in the same sense that we died in Christ. 2. The penalty of death threatened against Adam in the event of his transgression was not merely the dissolution of the body, but spiritual death, the loss of the divine favor and of original righteousness; and the consequent corruption of his whole nature. 3. This penalty came upon his race. His sin was the judicial ground on which the favor and fellowship of God were withdrawn or withheld from the apostate family of man. 4. Since the fall, therefore, men are by nature, or as they are born, the children of wrath. They are not only under condemnation, but destitute of original righteousness, and corrupted in their whole nature. According to this view of the subject, the ground of the imputation of Adam's sin is the federal union between him and his posterity, in such sense that it would not have been imputed had he not been constituted their representative. It is imputed to them not because it was antecedently to that imputation, and irrespective of the covenant on which the imputation is founded, already theirs; but because they were appointed to stand their probation in him.[40]

We all, therefore, sustain a twofold relationship to Adam. He is both our natural head and our federal representative. In all of his writings prior to the publication of the *Systematic Theology* in 1872 and 1873, Hodge insisted that it was on the grounds of the latter relationship, federal headship, that we are made liable to the penalty for Adam's sin, a penalty that consisted in the deprivation of righteousness, the suffering of inner corruption, and exposure to God's wrath. Hodge was forced to take this position because of his creationist views—namely, that the soul was not derived from the parents as the body is, but was given individually by divine fiat. The soul comes fresh from the hand of God and at the moment of birth becomes liable to punishment for Adam's sin. Some of Hodge's critics believed that this was a curious position for a Reformed divine to take, but it should be noted that Hodge could claim some company among the Reformed. It seems to court the idea that there is perhaps a moment of innocence in the life of each person before the sentence of guilt begins to be implemented. Furthermore, it reduces the idea of original sin to something less than Protestant theology has usually held out for; original sin, it seems, is not really an inherent corruption transmitted from parent to child, but a corruption inflicted upon people by God. The link is not a common nature, nor yet a universalized humanity, but a decree of God. To deny that we were in some sense acting in Adam through a common nature was to make the same denial that the Remonstrants had uttered. The belated concession by Hodge, then, that we are condemned not only because of federal representation but also because of natural relationship may have been an indication that the Princeton theologian realized some of the difficulties to which his theory was leading, but it is doubtful whether the concession alone, without any serious modifications to the entire doctrine, could save him from the charge, ironical as it was, that he had inadvertently espoused Arminian tenets.[41]

In view of this, it is necessary to examine in some detail the exegetical grounds on which Hodge's views of representation were built. The principal writing in which this is made plain is his *Commentary on the Epistle to the Romans*. It was no accident that Hodge chose to write on this letter. Both Moses Stuart and Albert Barnes produced commentaries on it and in the process slighted the view of immediate imputation espoused by Hodge.

In Romans 5:12-21, the central argument according to Hodge is contained in verses 12, 18, and 19, verses 13-17 being a parenthesis. This in itself cut across the grain of Barnes's and Stuart's argument, for it suggested that the passage did not intend to dwell on the disproportionate blessings of Christ's righteousness compared with the evils occasioned by the Fall. The apostle, rather, was arguing for the similarities between Adam's representative and Christ, not for their dissimilarities. The crux is verse 12, "As by the offence of one all are condemned, so by the righteousness of one are all justified," verses 18 and 19 being its amplification. The apostle sets out to show, however "contrary to the common mode of thinking among men," that God dealt with mankind in this representative. For if a penalty has been inflicted on men, a law must have been transgressed. Sin is not imputed where there is no transgressed law. The law in question, however, could not have been Moses' Law, since there were many who died before it was given (v. 14); it could not be nature's law written on the heart. Therefore, "as neither of these laws is sufficiently extensive to embrace *all* the subjects of the penalty, we must conclude that men are subject to death on account of Adam; that is, it is for the offence of one that many die, vs. 13, 14."[42] Thus is Adam a type of Christ.

The key to understanding the critical words in verse 12 is to understand the word *death* not in a physiological sense, but a penal one. In that case, the verse could be paraphrased thus: "All men are subject to penal evils on account of one man; this is the position to be proved, (v. 12) that such is the case is evident, because the infliction of a penalty supposes the violation of a law. But such evil was inflicted before the giving of the Mosaic law, it comes on men before the transgression of the law of nature, or even the existence of inherent depravity, it must, therefore, be for the offence of one man that judgment has come upon all them to condemnation."[43] Hodge maintained this causal link between Adam's sin and our condemnation without using the Augustinian device of translating the *eph' hō* as *in whom (in quo)*, in which case it would read: By one man all men became sinners, and hence death passed upon all men, *through that one man*, in whom all sinned. He settled for the simple statement "All die for that, or because that, all have sinned." He insisted, however, that the last phrase is to be interpreted as meaning that "all men are regarded and treated as sinners" on account of Adam's act. Interpretations that sever the causal link between Adam's act and God's subsequent treatment of mankind under conditions of condemnation are to be rejected. Thus Stuart suggested that the verse be rendered "As Adam sinned and died, so in like manner death has passed on all men, because all have sinned," and others proposed: "As by Adam, sin (corruption of nature) was introduced into the world, and death as its consequence, and so death passed on all men, because all have become corrupt." The point of this verse, Hodge countered, is not to contrast Adam and Christ, showing that corruption sprang from the one and holiness from the other, nor to show that Adam was the reason for our condemnation as Christ is for our justification. It is true that inner corruption comes from Adam, but this is neither the truth that is in view nor the basis on which God pronounces his judgment on us. Unless this is granted, the biblical doctrine of justification falls away.[44] Union with "Adam is the cause of death; union with Christ is the cause of life,"[45] and in both cases the principles of representation, of imputation, of federal union, are identical. In the one case human beings are treated as judicially guilty without respect to their actual condition, and in the other case Christians are treated as judicially innocent without respect to their actual condition.

That the ground of imputation of sin was man's federal relationship to Adam, rather than natural union, is clear from the fact that Jesus was part of Adam's natural posterity yet Adam's sin was not imputed to him. The fact that Jesus was regarded as sinless "supposes that the federal, and not the natural union is the essential ground of the imputation; that the sense in which Adam's sin is ours is a legal and not a moral sense and that the sense in which we sinned in him is that in which we act as a representative and not a literal sense."[46] Inner pollution was not transmitted to Christ, not because the Virgin Birth interrupted its transmission, but because Adam had not represented him and therefore God did not inflict him with this depravity.

The symmetry between the two Adams is almost perfect in Hodge's theology. We are justified and declared free from penal sanction not for what we do, but for what Christ did for us, just as we are declared liable to punishment not for what we have done, but for what Adam did as our representative. Hodge summarized his doctrine thus:

> 1. That Christ, in the covenant of redemption, is constituted the head and representative of his people, and that, in virtue of this federal union, and agreeably to the terms of the eternal covenant, they are regarded and treated as having done what he did and suffered what he suffered in their name and in their behalf. They died in him. They rose in him; not literally, so that his acts were their acts, but representatively. 2. That the reward promised to Christ in the covenant of redemption, was the justification, sanctification, and eternal salvation of his people. 3. That the judicial ground, therefore, of the justification of the believers is not their own personal righteousness, nor the holy nature which they derive from Christ, but his obedience and sufferings, performed and endured in their name, and which became theirs in virtue of the covenant and by gracious imputation of God. 4. That the believer is not only justified by the righteousness of Christ, but sanctified by his Spirit.[47]

The work of Christ, then, was centrally that of satisfying the demands of justice, thereby enabling God to be just when justifying sinners. To do this, Christ represented us in our sin, as a priest offering himself sacrificially in our stead. He bore our sin, propitiating the divine wrath that it called forth.

The atonement led naturally into considerations of theodicy, for Hodge believed that the justice of God required an atonement and the atonement made possible the preservation of the moral structure of the world. The character of God was on trial and remains on trial, for his justice demands that he treat his creatures as they deserve. If he is moral, he will favor what is good and show his disapprobation for what is wrong. This disapprobation, Hodge believed, is administered not merely as a deterrent to society, nor as a form of rehabilitation of the sinner, but because it is deserved. And because it is deserved, only Christ's interposition could preserve us from that calamity which the vindication of God's character would produce.

Here lay the crux, so to speak, of Hodge's differences with the New School thinkers. For they believed, in most cases, that in God's government of the world punishment was used but the purpose was to prevent sin and to correct the sinner. This attitude led naturally to the assumption that the chief goal of existence is happiness, and holiness is simply the best way to get there. But, countered Hodge, "we know that holiness is something more than a means; that to be happy is not the end and

reason for being holy; that enjoyment is not the highest end of being."
This results in our viewing ethical choices in commercial terms. A choice
is made, not because it is the inherently right thing to do, but because
it produces profit of some kind and avoids loss. Virtue becomes expe-
diency. The end justifies the means. And human beings are degraded
because their moral capacities are reduced to being merely the instru-
ments of happiness.

The debate between Hodge and Taylor represented the collision
between two entire theological systems. At the center of one was the
representative view of the atonement, of which Hodge was the chief
proponent, and at the center of the other was the governmental theory
whose most articulate advocate was Taylor. And related to each view
were different understandings of human nature and of God's moral relationship to the world.

Hodge's view was obviously constructed around a symmetry between the two Adams. This had the twofold advantage of providing a
cutting edge in the debate over human nature and placing justification
at the center of Christ's work, for both doctrines—that of sin and that
of justification—depended upon the idea of imputation. In the one,
Adam represents us covenantally, being the federal head of the race,
and in the other Christ represents us in his righteousness and through
that righteousness redeems us from the law's sanction, bearing it in
himself in our stead.

The parallel was not of course precise in every detail. The sin of
Adam, as Hodge came to stress, was not only imputed to us by means
of a sentence or declaration, it was also transmitted to us by nature. We
are sinners both by what we are and by what we did in Adam our head.
On the other hand, we are justified not by what we are—that is the
Roman Catholic view—but by what we are declared to be in Christ. The
chronology of these aspects, in other words, is not paralleled on the two
sides of the equation. The declaration of human sin followed after it,
whereas the declaration of the Christian's righteousness in Christ pre-
cedes its actual existence. In Hodge's thought, however, this parallelism
was greatly complicated by the fact that he was a creationist. This meant,
then, that the depravity of Adam was handed on to succeeding generations as much by divine decree as anything. This is quite unlike the
manner in which our actual righteousness is transmitted to us by Christ,
which occurs, not by divine decree, but by union with him.

Taylor's view was, of course, quite different. He opposed the view
of depravity as believed by Hodge and though he on occasion used the
word *imputation*, it was never in a Hodgean sense. The atonement was
for Taylor the ground upon which God could forgive sin. What, then,
was this ground? Was it that Christ bore the sin of those whom he

represented, suffering vicariously for them? Not at all. Rather, he held as had Grotius before him that an equivalent manifestation of God's justice is made in Christ's death. This means that the Cross was the occasion upon which God showed his general displeasure about sin. Having done so and thereby sustained his own moral government of the world, he had secured for himself, as it were, a free hand to forgive all or any without requiring of them a strict equivalent of punishment in Christ for sins committed.

This principle was taken a step further in Bushnell, who articulated a view held more or less in common with Auguste Sabatier, A. Ritschl, A. Harnack, Hastings Rashdall, and R. S. Franks. The essence of the idea, originally stated by Abelard, was that through the incarnation, God illumined the world by his wisdom and aimed to excite in us a love for him. The atonement is important, not for what was done objectively on the Cross, but for the *effect* that it has on us subsequently and subjectively; the atonement, in other words, takes place in and with the human response that it evokes. It is this principle that Bushnell clarified. Love, he said, provided the identity between God and sin; we do not look to the vinegar and gall and the writhing body of Jesus as the grounds for forgiveness, but to that divine love in the depths of which our sin is borne and absorbed. The Cross, therefore, is a declaration, not of the satisfaction of our sins in Christ, but of their cancellation within the being of God so that, having expressed his displeasure over sin and painfully accepted the consequences, his moral government of the world is still intact. But such a solution does mean that by grounding the principle of sacrifice solely in love, even if the character of God is magnified in the process, Bushnell leaves his readers with the impression that the work of Christ is not unique. There is, he says, a Gethsemane and a Calvary in *all* love, the mother who tearfully suffers over her child, the husband who mourns the premature death of his wife, those in the nation who sorrowfully bear in their spirits the weight of collective calamities and follies. Love, he declares, suffers the adversities and pains of others, taking on itself the burden of their evils. This is true not only of divine love, but also of human.

Nathaniel Taylor, therefore, represents a halfway house between Hodge and Bushnell. In Hodge the work of Christ, even if it has to be appropriated subjectively, is nevertheless firmly objective; in Bushnell it is largely subjective. In Hodge the law in accordance with which the universe runs is an expression of what God is; in Taylor and Bushnell there is more than a hint that this law is outside of God, and hence of itself arbitrary. In Hodge the work of Christ, relative to the expressed character of God, is unique; in Bushnell it is not.

Conclusion

It was Hodge's calling to live in a time of extraordinary intellectual transformation in the nation, a time when many of its structures and institutions were in disarray, and when the church itself was in some disorder and perplexity. The church stood at a crossroads, and Hodge pulled mightily in one direction while Taylor, aided by the changing climate in the country, pulled equally insistently in the other. They were both victorious. Hodge succeeded in excising the New School cancer from Presbyterian church life, but Taylor succeeded in opening the door to theological views that would soon spread far and wide and be the ruin of evangelical faith, Reformed and Arminian. Taylor was the stepping stone to the next generation's Liberalism, and that in turn would produce the countermovement of Fundamentalism. How very different subsequent American church life might have been if Hodge had prevailed in expunging Taylorism not only from Presbyterian circles but also from Protestantism in general! As it was, he slowed the inevitable march toward a theology resonant with human self-confidence, as was the culture, but he could not halt it.

It is not difficult to see Hodge's weaknesses. He was not a great historian; only when he was stiffly debated about his claims to historic Calvinism did he grudgingly allow that he believed many things Calvin never taught. He did not recognize as matters for serious theological reflection what was going on in the culture. His *Systematic Theology*, as a result, reads like a piece of eternal wisdom, albeit gathered from European divines, which could be deposited in any age or place with equal ease. He was more astute philosophically than his readers may realize, but he was prone to treat philosophy with the back of his hand. At the same time, he drew heavily off philosophical writers. He also imbibed the interests of Common Sense realism, which was, after all, an Enlightenment philosophy. This occurred almost without recognition on his part.

All of these things are true. But these weaknesses occurred within a man who at times almost alone held back the floodwaters of a sickly cultural theology and who, as a result, must be accorded a place in the annals of church history that cannot be erased. He was a man of very great integrity who followed single-mindedly his calling to obey the teaching of the biblical Word, and through this to live his life to God's glory. And in this he succeeded.

Notes: Charles Hodge

1. The creation of Princeton Theological Seminary had originally met with considerable resistance among ministers. Philip Lindsley spoke of the "popular

clamour [sic] so extensively raised against our school" because of the fear it would become "an engine of political power" and undercut the role of practicing ministers in training future ministers (Philip Lindsley, *A Plea for the Theological Seminary at Princeton, N.J.* [Trenton, 1821], 19, 18). Despite its successful establishment, as well as that of other seminaries, the preparation of ministers lagged far behind the need. Timothy Dwight, who was appointed President of Yale College in 1795, noted that between 1700 and 1801 the population had doubled every twenty-three years. In 1801, however, of 1,008 active churches in Massachusetts and Connecticut, only 749 had ministers. This pattern persisted through the nineteenth century. In 1828, the *Journal of the American Education Society* reported that among 960 Congregational churches, 240 had pastoral vacancies; among 3,723 Calvinistic Baptist churches, 1,146 were vacant; among the Protestant Episcopal churches 112 of the 598 churches were vacant. The next year Hodge reported that between 600 and 700 Presbyterian congregations out of 1,880 were "destitute of regular pastors," and he went on to note that "the proportion of ministers, to the population of the United States, is every year rapidly diminishing" (Anon. [Charles Hodge], *Articles on the American Education Society* [Philadelphia, 1928], 7). In 1846 the American Home Missionary Society issued a "loud call" for men for the West and South; Ohio needed 11, Indiana 14, Michigan 13, Wisconsin 11, Illinois 16, Missouri 9, Iowa 10, Georgia 2, Kentucky 4, Tennessee 2 (*Thirtieth Annual Report of the Directors of the American Education Society* [Boston, 1846], 47). The fear that Hodge expressed, that the proportion of ministers relative to the population was declining, was paralleled in some figures Ebenezer Porter published in 1821. In his survey of college graduates, he had found that between 1620 and 1720, approximately 1 in 2 became ministers; between 1720 and 1770, the proportion dropped to 1 in 3; between 1770 and 1810 to 1 in 5; and between 1800 and 1810 to 1 in 6 (Ebenezer Porter, *A Sermon Delivered in Boston, on the Anniversary of the American Education Society* [Andover, 1921], 5).

    2. Earl William Kennedy, "An Historical Analysis of Charles Hodge's Doctrines of Sin and Particular Grace" (Ph.D. diss., Princeton Theological Seminary, 1968), 17.

    3. Timothy Dwight, *A Discourse on Some Events of the Last Century, Delivered in the Brick Church in New Haven, on Wednesday, January 7, 1801* (New Haven, 1801), 23. Cf. Dwight's attitude to·vard the French Revolution in his *The Major Poems of Timothy Dwight (1752-1817), With a Dissertation on the History, Eloquence, and Poetry of the Bible* (Gainesville, FL: Scholars' Facsimiles and Reprints, 1969), 384.

    4. Dwight, *A Discourse*, 19.

    5. Joseph Lathrop, *A Sermon, on the Dangers of the Times, from Infidelity and Immorality; and Especially from a Lately Discovered Conspiracy Against Religion and Government, Delivered at West Springfield and afterward at Springfield* (Springfield, 1798), 12.

    6. Characteristic assessments are found in Lyman Beecher, *A Sermon, Delivered in the North Presbyterian Church in Hartford, May 20, 1813, On the Evening Subsequent to the Formation of the "Connecticut Society for the Promotion of Good Morals"* (Hartford, 1813); R. D. Mussey, *An Address on Ardent Spirit, Read Before the New Hampshire Medical Society at their Annual Meeting, June 5, 1827 and Published at their Request* (Boston, 1929); Leonard Bacon, *Total Abstinence from Ardent Spirits, An Address Delivered by Request of the Young Men's Temperance Society of New-Haven, in the North Church, June 24, 1829* (New-Haven, 1829); James Dana,

The Folly of Practical Atheism. A Discourse Delivered in the Chapel of Yale College, on Lord's Day, November 23, 1794 (New-Haven, 1794).

7. Horace Bushnell, *Crisis in the Church* (Hartford, 1835).

8. Thomas Belsham, *American Unitarianism; or a Brief History of "the Progress and Present State of the Unitarian Churches in America," Compiled from Documents, and Information Communicated by the Rev. James Freeman, D. D. and William Wells Jun. Esq. of Boston, and From Other Unitarian Gentlemen in this Country, by Rev. Thomas Belsham. Extracted from His "Memories of the Life of the Reverend Theophilus Lindsey," Printed in London, 1812, and Now Published for the Benefit of the Christian Churches in this Country, without Note or Alteration* (Boston, 1815). Jedediah Morse and Jeremiah Evarts, "Review of American Unitarianism," *Panoplist* 11 (June 1815): 241-72.

9. William E. Channing, *A Letter to the Rev. Samuel C. Thatcher, on the Aspersions Contained in a Late Number of the Panoplist on the Ministers of Boston and the Vicinity* (Boston, 1815); Noah Worcester, *A Letter to the Rev. William E. Channing on the Subject of His Letter to the Rev. Samuel Thatcher* (Boston, 1815); William E. Channing, *Remarks on the Rev. Dr. Worcester's Letter to Mr. Channing, on the "Review of American Unitarianism"* (Boston, 1815); Noah Worcester, *A Second Letter to the Rev. William E. Channing on the Subject of Unitarianism* (Boston, 1815); William E. Channing, *Remarks on the Rev. Dr. Worcester's Second Letter to Mr. Channing on American Unitarianism* (Boston, 1815); Noah Worcester, *A Third Letter to the Rev. William E. Channing on the Subject of Unitarianism* (Boston, 1815).

10. [B. B. Wisner], *A Review of the Rev. Dr. Channing's Discourse, Preached at the Dedication of the Second Congregational Unitarian Church, New York, December 7, 1826* (Boston, 1827), 4.

11. William E. Channing, *A Sermon Delivered at the Ordination of the Rev. Jared Sparks, to the Pastoral Care of the First Independent Church in Baltimore, May 5, 1819* (Baltimore, 1819).

12. Moses Stuart, *Letters to the Rev. Wm. E. Channing, Containing Remarks on his Sermon, Recently Preached and Published at Baltimore* (Andover, 1819); [Andrews Norton], *A Statement of Reasons For Not Believing the Doctrines of Trinitarians Respecting the Nature of God, and the Person of Christ. Occasioned By Professor Stuart's Letters to Mr. Channing* (Boston, 1819); Leonard Woods, *Letters to Unitarians Occasioned by the Sermon of the Reverend William E. Channing at the Ordination of the Rev. J. Sparks* (Andover, 1820); Henry Ware, *Letters Addressed to Trinitarians and Calvinists, Occasioned by Dr. Woods' Letters to Unitarians* (Cambridge, 1820); Leonard Woods, *A Reply to Dr. Ware's Letters to Trinitarians and Calvinists* (Andover, 1821); Henry Ware, *Answer to Dr. Woods' Reply, In a Second Series of Letters Addressed to Trinitarians and Calvinists* (Cambridge, 1822); Leonard Woods, *Remarks on Dr. Ware's Answer* (Andover, 1822); Henry Ware, *A Postscript to the Second Series of Letters Addressed to Trinitarians and Calvinists, In Reply to the Remarks of Dr. Woods on those Letters* (Cambridge, 1823).

13. Samuel Miller, *Letters on Unitarianism; Addressed to the Members of the First Presbyterian Church, in the City of Baltimore* (Trenton, 1821). Cf. Moses Stuart, *Letters on the Eternal Generation of the Son of God, addressed to the Rev. Samuel Miller, D. D.* (Andover, 1822); Samuel Miller, *Letters on the Eternal Sonship of Christ: addressed to the Rev. Prof. Stuart, of Andover* (Philadelphia, 1823). Archibald Alexander, "Remarks on Correspondence between Prof. Stuart and Doc. Miller," MS, File D, Speer Memorial Library, Princeton Theological Seminary.

14. Lyman Beecher, *The Autobiography of Lyman Beecher*, ed. Barbara M. Cross, 2 vols. (Cambridge, 1961), 1:430.

15. Ibid., 1:400.

16. Ibid., 2:11.

17. Anon., Review of *The Atonement: Discourses and Treatises by Edwards, Smalley, Maxy, Emmons, Griffin, Burge, and Weeks. With an Introductory Essay by Edwards A. Park, The Congregational Quarterly* 1 (July 1859): 309.

18. An Edwardsean [Joseph Harvey?], *Letters, On the Present State and Probable Results of Theological Speculations in Connecticut* (no publication information), 27-28.

19. A Presbyterian, *A Critical, Philosophical, and Theological Review of A Dissertation on Native Depravity, by Gardiner Spring, D. D.* (New York, 1833), 9.

20. Charles Hodge, Review of *A Brief History and Vindication of the Doctrines received and established in the Churches of New England,* by Thomas Clap, *The Biblical Repertory and Princeton Review* 11 (July 1839): 369-404.

21. An Observer [N. Hewit?], *An Address, to the Congregational Churches in Connecticut, on the Present State of Their Religious Concerns* (Hartford, 1933), 17.

22. Charles Hodge, "Remarks on the Princeton Review," *The Biblical Repertory and Princeton Review* 23 (1851): 309.

23. Andrews Norton, "Thoughts on True and False Religion," *Christian Disciple* 2, new series (1820): 337-65; [Nathaniel Taylor], "Review of Eskine's Evidences, and Norton on True and False Religion," *The Quarterly Christian Spectator* 4 (1822): 249-64, 299-318, 445-48, 667-68; Andrews Norton, "Views of Calvinism," *Christian Disciple* 4, new series (1822): 244-80; [Nathaniel Taylor], "Review of Norton's Views of Calvinism," *The Quarterly Christian Spectator* 5 (1823): 196-224; Anon., "The State of the Calvinistic Controversy," *Christian Disciple* 5, new series (May and June 1823): 212-35; Anon. [Nathaniel Taylor], "Review Renewed," *The Quarterly Christian Spectator* 6 (1824): 310-37, 360-74.

24. Anon. [Nathaniel Taylor], "Review Renewed," 301.

25. Anon. [Nathaniel Taylor], "Review of Norton's . . . ," 217.

26. Ibid.

27. Leonard Bacon, "Future Punishment of Infants Not a Doctrine of Calvinism," *Spirit of the Pilgrims* 1 (January 1828): 45-52; "Future Punishment of Infants Not a Doctrine of Calvinism," *Spirit of the Pilgrims* 1 (February 1828): 78-95; and "Future State of Infants," *Spirit of the Pilgrims* 1 (March 1828): 149-64. Lyman Beecher, "To the Editor of the Christian Examiner and Theological Review," *Spirit of the Pilgrims* 3 (January 1830): 17-24; "To the Editor of the Christian Examiner and Theological Review," *Spirit of the Pilgrims* 3 (February 1830): 72-86; "To the Editor of the Christian Examiner and Theological Review," *Spirit of the Pilgrims* 3 (April 1830): 181-95. Cf. "Examination of a Note by Dr. Beecher," *The Christian Examiner* 4 (September and October 1827): 431-48; 5 (May and June 1828): 229-63.

28. Beecher, *Autobiography,* 1:410.

29. Ibid., 2:158.

30. Ibid., 2:159.

31. Anon., "Beecher's Sermon at Worcester," *The Christian Examiner* 1 (January and February 1824): 49-50.

32. Anon., "On the State of the Question Between the Orthodox and Liberal Parties in This Country," *The Christian Examiner* 5 (January and February 1828): 1.

33. Charles Hodge, "General Assembly of 1837," *The Biblical Repertory and Princeton Review* 9 (July 1837): 407-85. Cf. Charles Hodge, "Reunion of Old and

New-School Presbyterians," *The Biblical Repertory and Princeton Review* 37 (April 1865): 271-313.

34. Leonard Bacon, *Seven Letters to the Rev. George A. Calhoun, Concerning the Pastoral Union of Connecticut, and its Charges Against the Ministers and Churches* (New Haven, 1840), 20.

35. Charles Hodge, "The New Divinity Tried," in *Theological Essays: Reprinted from the Princeton Review* (New York, 1846), 12.

36. See Elwyn A. Smith, "The Doctrine of Imputation and the Presbyterian Schism of 1837-38," *Journal of the Presbyterian Historical Society* 38 (September 1960): 129-51.

37. Charles Hodge, "What is Christianity?" *The Biblical Repertory and Princeton Review* 32 (January 1860): 137.

38. Ibid.

39. See Peter Y. DeJong, *The Covenant Idea in New England Theology 1620-1847* (Grand Rapids, 1945).

40. Charles Hodge, "The First and Second Adam," *The Biblical Repertory and Princeton Review* 32 (April 1860): 340.

41. The Reformers included under the term *original sin* both what was inherited and what was imputed. The distinction between original sin and original damnation was to come later. Hodge's opponents saw in his position such a stress on imputation, hence on original damnation, that current corruption was not adequately affirmed. This objection took several forms. Goodrich in his debate with Hodge, carried in *The Christian Quarterly Spectator*, sought to embarrass Hodge on this point, arguing that "by insisting that *reatus* denotes mere *liability to punishment* rather than ill-desert (true guilt), [Hodge] has unwittingly espoused the position which Turretin ascribes to the Remonstrants, and which he attacks as really a denial of imputation" (Kennedy, "Charles Hodge's Doctrines of Sin and Particular Grace," 73). Later, Robert Dabney charged that Hodge's insistence on parallels in every detail between the representation of the two Adams led naturally to Arminianism and Romanism. On the latter point, justification would have to be seen as an infused righteousness to correspond to the infused corruption, and on the former point, faith must precede and not follow regeneration: "Every one who has a *modicum* of theological knowledge knows that this is precisely Arminianism" (Robert L. Dabney, "Hodge's Systematic Theology," *The Southern Presbyterian Review* 24 [1873]: 209). Along a slightly different line, Landis argued that Hodge undercut, with his insistence on this parallel between the Adams, an actual participation in Adam's sin. For Hodge, he thought, there was only imputed sin and not actual participation in Adam in his sinning (R. L. Landis, " 'Unthinkable' Propositions and Original Sin," *The Southern Presbyterian Review* 26 [April 1875]: 313-15). This charge was developed fully in his book *The Doctrine of Original Sin, as Received and Taught by the Churches of the Reformation, Stated and Defended, and the Error of Dr. Hodge in Claiming that this Doctrine Recognizes the Gratuitous Imputation of Sin, Pointed Out and Refuted* (Richmond, 1884).

42. Charles Hodge, *Commentary on the Epistle to the Romans* (Philadelphia, 1864), 176.

43. Ibid., 190.

44. Ibid., 185.

45. Charles Hodge, *Systematic Theology*, 3 vols. (New York, 1872), 2:203.

46. Hodge, "The First and Second Adam," 367.

47. Ibid., 340-41.

3

BENJAMIN B. WARFIELD

W. ANDREW HOFFECKER

Benjamin B. Warfield

When Benjamin B. Warfield was called from Western Seminary in Pittsburgh to Princeton Seminary in 1887, the Seminary had been an established and dominant force for over seventy years. He joined a succession of professors that included Archibald Alexander, Charles Hodge, and his son A. A. Hodge, who were influential in training over six thousand students in Christian theology.[1] Warfield occupied the chair of Didactic and Polemical Theology. His task at Princeton, like his predecessors', was to produce ministers who were so thoroughly trained in Reformed theology that they could effectively proclaim the gospel and refute any teaching that did not conform to the high standard of Calvinistic orthodoxy.

Warfield's legacy at Princeton was a proud tradition. As Archibald Alexander, Princeton's first president, approached death, he summoned Charles Hodge to his bedside and gave him a walking stick. This stick, explained Alexander, was handed down to Hodge "as a symbol of orthodoxy."[2] The elder Hodge fulfilled that theological mission by his dedicated leadership of Old School Presbyterians, his voluminous publications, and his diligent seminary teaching. Charles's son, A. A. Hodge, filled the chair of theology for only seven years after his father's death in 1878. Although the younger Hodge's premature death prevented him from attaining the stature of his father, his *Outlines of Theology* has been recognized by some followers of Princeton as a model of theological precision. Also, in his *Popular Lectures on Theological Themes,* published posthumously in 1887, Hodge articulated as forcefully as any of the other Princeton men a Calvinistic basis for the integration of Christianity with cultural activity. And when nineteenth-century secularists mounted campaigns for religious activity in American public life, Hodge urgently insisted that Calvinism was the only theological worldview from which Christians could defend traditional American values and institutions such as family, law, education, and economics.

Of course, in many academic circles today, theological wags would sarcastically whisper that Warfield's appointment perpetuated an already ingrown theological atmosphere. Their criticism would be that instead of adding diversity of opinion, the party line simply gained yet another advocate. But the Princetonians considered their tradition a sacred trust; they gloried in their Reformed heritage. And Warfield's appointment certainly enhanced their efforts through writing and lecturing to maintain orthodoxy's influence in American religious life. In a remark long remembered and often berated by Princeton's detractors, Charles Hodge twice publicly claimed that "a new idea never originated" at Princeton. Those sympathetic to Reformed theology echoed his words, interpreting them to mean that although scholarly research went forward, no modification of belief resulted. Not only did Princetonians deny adjusting their message to suit their times, but they also staunchly resisted any attempt to move Presbyterianism from its Calvinist moorings.

In fact, at the seminary's 1912 centennial celebration, Francis L. Patton proudly claimed that Princeton theology "is exactly the same as it was a hundred years ago." He added that while there has been a New Haven Theology and an Andover Theology, "there never was a distinctively Princeton Theology; Princeton's boast, if she has any reason to boast at all, is in her unwavering fidelity to the theology of the Reformation."[3] Hodge's and Patton's claims have been the object of much debate between old Princeton's friends and critics alike. Ned B. Stonehouse, as a sympathetic biographer of one of Princeton's revered professors, J. Gresham Machen, pointedly argues that Hodge's and Warfield's theologies were not "at every point as completely free of philosophical and speculative influences as they wanted to be and supposed they were—or as lacking in originality as they seemed to claim." Yet he qualified his remarks by saying that any noticeable change in emphasis was due to a "new note of militancy as the issues were drawn . . . in America and Europe."[4]

The purpose of this chapter is to evaluate several of Warfield's major contributions to the Princeton theology in light of discussions about continuity and discontinuity in thought among the various men. Even though Warfield produced no *magnum opus*, he wrote hundreds of articles and reviews that provide ample material by which both the broad outlines and the details of his views may be judged. This chapter will examine three areas that reflect concerns not only prominent in Warfield's work but stressed by his Princeton predecessors as well: religious experience, scholarly criticism in academic journals, and the use of Scottish Common Sense Philosophy. Warfield's predecessors had already articulated clear positions on each of these subjects. A commitment to preserve an established tradition was foremost in each of their minds, yet a changing historical context brought radical changes in the late nineteenth and early twentieth centuries. Liberal theological trends from Europe were threatening to dislodge not only Princeton's Reformed theology but evangelical theology as a whole.[5] Therefore, Warfield's views of the religious life, the theologian's academic task, and rational defense of the faith will be seen against the backdrop of a changing intellectual and cultural milieu.

Religious Experience: Private Piety and Cultural Transformation

Mark A. Noll has provided a revealing account of what concerns motivated Presbyterians to found a seminary in the opening years of the nineteenth century. In "The Founding of Princeton Seminary,"[6] he points out that Christian experience joined with sound theology was stressed at Princeton Seminary from its very inception in 1812. In fact, when Ashbel Green drafted his plan for the Seminary, he not only included a "plan of governance," but he also stipulated that academic study and spiritual nurture together were to form the foundation of ministerial training. Students were expected to explain and defend the Bible and to cultivate vital Christian piety. Princeton's founders wanted a learned clergy who could answer speculations posed by deism and unbelief and a respectable clergy who could bring stability to a newly formed and restless political order. But these founders also demanded a "pious clergy" whose spiritual influence could combat religion's loss of influence, which was threatening to engulf American society. In previous works I have attempted to show the Princetonians' desire and labors to fulfill this charge.[7] Not wanting merely to repeat conclusions of these studies, I believe that further clarification of what Warfield attempted is in order.

Writing in a popular journal, *The Presbyterian Messenger*, in 1896, Warfield explicitly stated his conception of how religious experience was to be related to theology. The conservative view that religion was the product of theology was being radically eclipsed among theological writers by liberals who reversed this relationship. By positing truth prior to both theology and experience, Warfield successfully sidestepped this recurring debate in which conservatives charged that liberals had subjectivized theology and liberals claimed that conservatives intellectualized religious experience. To Warfield, such disputation was fruitless. "Neither," he claimed, "is the product of the other, but both are products of religious truth, operative in the two spheres of life and thought."[8] Warfield's intention, however, was not to probe a dichotomous phenomenon—head versus heart, intellect versus feeling—as he was most wont to do in discussions of theology and religious experience. Instead he enumerated *three* "media" or "channels of communication"—authority, intellect, and heart—all three of which must relate harmoniously as the bases of both religion and theology. Each of these channels may plausibly be argued as the basis for the religious life and theological formulation. For example, he stated that by authority one knows "only what and as God tells." God's truth is also clearly "addressed to the intellect." Yet someone might contend that "our upward strivings, our feeling of dependence and responsibility supply the points of contact between us and God."[9]

But any simplified reduction of religion and theology ends in distortion. Exaggeration of authority yields traditionalistic dogmatism that renders mute the heart and intellect. Stressing intellect, on the other hand, results in rationalistic system building based on "*a priori* fancies" which system in turn precludes any authoritative claims of God's Word or of human conscience.[10] Finally, following only the heart renders one susceptible to mysticism that will bow to no authoritative word or rational thought, but only to "currents of feeling which flow up and down in our souls," giving birth to "competing revelations" and worshiping "the most morbid of human imaginations."[11] True to his Augustinian heritage, Warfield proposed that dangers can be avoided by following another great trinity similar to those enumerated by the famous early church father. Authority, intellect, and heart are the three sides of "the triangle of truth," which can be diagrammed as follows:

God's authoritative Word initiates both the religious life and theology.

Christian experience converts the soul and produces power for an obedient life.

Christian theology converts the soul and leads the renewed mind to receive spiritual things from the Spirit of God.

The unified triangle represents Warfield's belief that authority, intellect, and heart are unified under God's truth. He contended that Scripture is not, therefore, merely grist for the theologians' systematizing mill. It is also life-producing nourishment for the soul. To change the metaphor, it both "enlightens" the mind and "beautifies" the heart. God's truth reaches its final end not merely by being assembled and organized into a theological system. Scripture is only fully "understood," Warfield claimed, when it is "lived." Fittingly, he concluded with the Augustinian motto "Believe that you may understand," which is taken from Isaiah 9:7: "Unless you believe, you will not understand." An individual has intellectually apprehended the truth only when he displays a corresponding power in his religious experience. True theology, shaped by a sanctified intellect, is always inextricably united with vital religion motivated by an instructed heart.[12]

If this triangle of truth was the model for Reformed religion and theology, how consistently were religion and theology integrated by Warfield at Princeton Seminary? From its earliest days until its reorganization in 1929, weekly conferences were held on Sunday afternoons to discuss practical religion. In two of Warfield's most memorable conference talks, he spoke on seminarians' cultivation of the religious life.[13] Two points stand out in both addresses. First, Warfield admitted that at Princeton students could easily feel compelled to emphasize academics over piety. He cited an interesting story, however, related by the famous Episcopal clergyman Phillips Brooks of Trinity Church, Boston, that illustrated the opposite emphasis at another seminary. Because he had never attended a prayer meeting before, Brooks almost despaired during his first evening devotions at seminary when he could not pray with the fervent spirit of his peers. Yet the next day he was amazed that the same students who had prayed so piously the previous evening displayed a woeful lack of preparation for their first Greek class recitation. Warfield candidly commented: "Well, it was not at Princeton Seminary that Dr. Brooks saw these evils!"[14]

Since the Princeton ideal had always been scholarship accompanied by piety, the greatest danger confronting theological students was not the lack of religion or theology but the tendency to view the two as antithetical.[15] With the same deliberation used in discussing the "triangle of truth" (i.e., by refusing to give priority to authority, intellect, or heart) in "Spiritual Culture in the Seminary" Warfield ascribed equal importance to devotion, intellectual training, and practical experience. "If intellectual acuteness will not of itself make a man an acceptable minister of Christ, neither will facility and energy in practical affairs by themselves, nor yet piety and devotion alone. The three must be twisted together into a single three-ply cord."[16]

Second, Warfield exhorted students to cultivate both corporate and individual piety. By temperament Warfield was more inclined to stress the latter over the former;[17] therefore, his inclusion of an extended discussion on "public means of grace" is all the more significant. He emphasized that the seminary provided several opportunities for formal gatherings: weekly worship on Sunday, conferences on practical religion, and daily prayer at the conclusion of each day. In addition classes were opened by prayer and monthly prayer meetings were organized for missions.[18]

A second part of Warfield's emphasis on corporate religious life was his challenge for students to be motivated by a theology of organic church life while they were still students. Every group of seminarians, he explained:

> bound in as close and intimate association as we are, must have an organic life; and if the bonds that bind them together are fundamentally of a religious character, this organic life must be fundamentally a religious one. . . . No richness of private religious life, no abundance of voluntary religious services [i.e., in "voluntary" movements in society] on the part of members of the organism, can take the place of or supersede the necessity for the fullest, richest, and most fervent expression of this organic religious life through its appropriate channels. I exhort you, therefore, brethren . . . to utilize the public means of grace afforded by the seminary and to make them instruments for the cultivation and expression of the organic religious life of the institution.[19]

So important is participation in the seminary's public means of grace that Warfield said, "The entire work of the seminary deserves to be classed in the category of the means of grace,"[20] and he attributed to it the power of penetrating much more deeply into the foundation of their religious natures than activity in voluntary societies and other forms of public service. He also asked students quite pointedly: "Shall you have everything also [i.e., dormitory life, classroom studies, etc.] in common except worship?" If they had been separated from their normal family and church life, should they not form a "religious community, with its own organic religious life and religious expression?"[21] One might expect a proposal for a "religious order" to follow!

Using these probing questions, Warfield attempted to broaden the focus of Princeton piety, since its adherents usually viewed religon as a private, individualistic walk with God. In these two conference talks Warfield challenged seminarians to appreciate the significance of the visible church and participate in its life. Unfortunately, Warfield never explained in greater detail how to implement his vision of seminary corporate religion. How should students integrate community and private life beyond attending formal worship and maintaining individual devotions? What biblical materials as well as writings in church history stress public worship as a means of grace? And what role should the sacraments play in both corporate and private life? Of course these questions might be addressed by other seminary departments that dealt directly with practical theology, but Warfield's lack of attention to them is regrettable. Perhaps his own predisposition to private piety was too strong, and he could not ever fully overcome it. Nevertheless, the fact that Warfield mentioned these matters is significant in light of his prescient remarks about the future character of religious institutions: "Without at least this much common worship [i.e., common prayer in morning and evening and formal gatherings twice on every Sabbath] I do not think the institution can preserve its character as a distinctively religious institution."[22] Today Warfield's words are an appropriate warning for seminary trustees and administrators since one of their most difficult challenges at the end of the twentieth century is the recovery of spirituality. "Spiritual formation" has become a priority at many seminaries where leaders now perceive a danger in viewing ministerial training solely as an academic discipline.

Warfield's view of the religious life also affected how he viewed the believer's relation to the broader culture. But not all his predecessors agreed with his emphasis. Although Princeton Seminary was founded largely to stem the rising tide of unbelief in American culture, its founders and early leaders sought to combat these evils primarily through constructing and defending sound theology. Little stress was placed on cultural reformation.[23] Such a generalization was defensible in Princeton's founders and early leaders. However, it was least true of Warfield's immediate predecessor, A. A. Hodge. Among Princeton's theologians, the younger Hodge articulated most compellingly the Christian responsibility to implement cultural change. In one of his popular lectures Hodge took umbrage at secularists' campaigns to introduce religious neutrality into American public life and uttered a solemn pronouncement that intellectual and spiritual integrity requires Christians "to bring all the action of the political society to which they belong obedient to the revealed will of Christ the supreme King, the Ruler among the nations."[24] Hodge ended his lecture by surveying civilization from the Flood to his own day and concluding not only that America completes Christianity's westward expansion, but also that Christianity's phenomenal growth confirms its destiny to exercise moral and religious leadership in the world. God's challenge to this generation is to use its vantage point at "the pyramid top of opportunity on which God has set us [to view] forty centuries!" Christianity's commission is to "stretch our hand into the future with power to mould the destinies of millions."[25]

Despite the fact that Warfield succeeded Hodge at a time when secularization had infiltrated much of American life,[26] he did not emphasize Christian commitment to cultural renewal as strongly as the younger Hodge. But neither did he exclude it altogether. In fact, Christians' cultural responsibility appears more frequently in his writings than might be expected. His review of Herman Bavinck's *De Zekerheid des*

Geloofs recounts in some detail Bavinck's criticism of "pietistic legalism," Moravianism, and Methodism for their failure to acknowledge God's sovereign purpose in public as well as private life. Warfield quotes approvingly an extended passage that bears remarkable resemblance to Hodge's view of Christ's Kingdom:

> The earthly spheres of art and science, of literature and politics, of domestic and social economy are underestimated in value and significance by them, and are consequently not reformed and regenerated by the Christian principle. To "rest in the wounds of Jesus" or "to be converted and then go forth to convert others" seems to constitute the entire content of the Christian life.[27]

By limiting piety to "sentimentality and unhealthy emotion" and "excitement and zeal without knowledge" Moravians and Methodists avoid discharging their Christian vocation in everyday life. "The open eye, the wide outlook, the expanded heart—these things do not come to their rights."[28] In a word, he emphasized, Christianity so considered has lost its "leaven."[29] Warfield was not merely mouthing Bavinck's emphasis. His deep personal conviction is evident from his challenge reminiscent of Hodge's decades earlier: Reformed Christians call for "the reformation of the world after the plan of God and its gradual transmutation into his Kingdom in which his will shall be done even as in heaven."[30]

Warfield's advocacy of Christian cultural responsibility developed from his admiration of Calvin's broad influence in the Reformation. Frequently he linked Calvin's name to the growth of free institutions in the West. In *The Methodist Review* Warfield claims that by freeing the Genevan church Calvin created the Protestant Church and instilled a spirit in his followers "to the efflourescence of which this modern world of ours owes its free institutions."[31] But Calvin's foremost contribution to Western culture was education. Due to Calvin's influence three theological schools opened in France. Peasants in Scotland rose higher in their economic status than their counterparts in other countries. But the prime example of Calvinists' pervasive use of education to raise the general cultural level is Puritanism in America. The Puritan educational system "is opening up a new era of human history."[32] He also defends the Genevan Reformer against oft-repeated charges that Calvin depreciated art. Rather than condemning art, Warfield answered, Calvin argued for a "pure and reverent employment of art as a high gift of God, to be used like all others of God's gifts so as to profit man and glorify the Great Giver."[33]

Finally, he contrasted Calvin's holistic perspective on the Christian life with Martin Luther's tendency to limit the Christian vision to an individual sense of sin and justification. Calvin's interests were broader, resulting in a religious worldview encompassing all of life, public and private. Besides the redemption of individuals, Calvin envisioned in Geneva a redeemed social life. He summarizes the Reformed worldview as one that "begins . . . centers . . . and ends with the vision of God in His glory; and it sets itself before all things to render to God His rights in every sphere of life-activity."[34]

How seriously Warfield took the Reformed vision by attempting in his own calling as a Christian scholar to influence American culture is indicated by two essays published in 1888 and 1889. Because he was born and raised in Kentucky he wrote self-consciously as a southern Christian addressing the church's responsibility to recently freed American blacks. His proposals are quite striking considering Warfield's reputation as a conservative. Since Christians know "that God has made of one blood all the nations of the earth" and has invested them with "the missionary spirit," their task is to "serve as the hand of the Most High in elevating the lowly and rescuing the oppressed."[35] Warfield even asked whether it is "good public policy" to compact a lower class and thus continue a social system that allows a class to have heaped on it "year after year, petty injustices and insults."[36]

Convinced that secular training alone was insufficient to the task and that merely preaching a spiritual gospel that does not motivate concrete action in the public life is ineffectual, Warfield called for Christian schools staffed by teachers with missionary zeal to educate believers on how to heal this social evil. He closed with a question directed not at individuals but at his denomination: "Can the Presbyterian Church safely neglect to do her part in this great work?"[37]

His second essay, "Drawing the Color Line," challenged America's churches even more directly. In this essay he complains that so little has been accomplished for the blacks since the Civil War[38] and that even ecclesiastical bodies had succumbed to the political suggestion that only racial segregation would prevent future racial antipathy. He criticized denominations for debating about "drawing the color line" and creating separate white and black groups within their ecclesiastical bodies. Warfield argued against a proposal in the Presbyterian Church by which the General Assembly is "willing to buy reunion with its Southern brethren at the fearful cost of affixing an unjust stigma" on the blacks.[39] The results, he predicted, would only be future racial conflict. Although Warfield's unpopular proposals went unheeded, they clearly reflected his contention that Christian piety definitely should result both in changed individual attitudes toward blacks and in active efforts to integrate public life. Obviously some might argue that his support of blacks was out of character with his traditional private and individualistic piety. But Warfield's prophetic public rebuke of American Christians exemplified his own desire to use biblical principles to challenge trends in the culture and improve it by concerted Christian action.[40]

Conservative Reaction to Nineteenth-Century Scholarship

Contemporary historians of American religion have not recognized Warfield's substantial contributions in their surveys. Typically Hodge has received more attention than any of the other Princeton theologians. Sydney Ahlstrom in *A Religious History of the American People* mentions Hodge four times[41] and Warfield but once. In Ahlstrom's words, Warfield brought "great theological and historical prowess to the defense of the Reformed tradition." His interests in "Reformed doctrine and Biblical inerrancy provided a major theme in the 'Fundamentalist Controversy' that raged within Northern Presbyterianism."[42]

Summarizing Warfield's contribution simply in terms of defense and advocacy of Reformed theology and biblical authority has much in its favor. But those who notice only these two categories ignore the breadth of his interests and the sheer volume of his writings. Most scholars overlook his extensive reviews in various journals, primarily the *Princeton Theological Review*. No major movement or writer in Europe or in America escaped his notice. From the 1830s to the 1870s Old School Presbyterians faithfully read Charles Hodge's views of Charles Finney's revivalism and the theologies of New Haven and Mercersburg, and eagerly awaited the July issue of the *Biblical Repertory and Theological Review* to devour his carefully prepared assessment of business and debate at the General Assembly. Because Warfield was unable to leave the Princeton area due to his caring for his invalid wife, he could not continue Hodge's reportage of denominational affairs. Instead, he kept Americans abreast of contemporary liberal scholarship through his indefatigable writing of reviews in journals.[43]

Content to allow Hodge's voluminous *Systematic Theology* to remain as the fundamental statement of Princeton's views,[44] Warfield focused his energies on writing articles and reviews for periodicals, journals, dictionaries, and the popular press.[45] Warfield's numerous reviews testify to the tremendous pressure conservatives felt to respond to the flood of scholarly works written by liberals who advocated radical change in the study of religion and Christianity. His review articles show Warfield the scholar "in the trenches" fighting not only to fend off foes of his beloved Reformed theology but also to defend doctrines dear to conservatives of every theological stripe. Supernaturalism itself was being repudiated by scholars who believed that the academic study of religion should be treated just as "objectively" as any other academic discipline; that is, it should be subjected to accepted scholarly canons of "neutral" judgment. Radical critics denied the Western tradition of treating Christianity as the uniquely revealed religion. Instead it was just one religion among others, and scholars were to study its origins, doctrines, history, and influence with the same detached scientific method they used in examining the world's other major faiths.

Thus Warfield's struggles were with several factions: radical scholars who denied the supernatural and wanted to reinterpret Christianity on naturalistic terms, and liberals who wanted to alter basic Christian doctrines in less varying degrees. Since the former were making significant inroads in Germany, Warfield most frequently devoted his exceptional powers of analysis and erudition to prevent their ideas from gaining acceptance in America.

What immediately strikes the reader is Warfield's candid assessment of each work he reviewed. When confronting the most capable radical critics, he genuinely praised their intellectual gifts and scholarly acumen while he scorchingly derided the paucity of their radical presuppositions. For example, Warfield expressed sincere appreciation for the scholarship of the Tübingen School:

> There is no student of the New Testament who will not confess deep indebtedness to the work of [Ferdinand Christian] Baur, for example, both for facts in abundance and for generalizations and points of view of the most stimulating character.[46]

Critiquing the famous German church historian Adolf Harnack's *History of Dogma*, he said that it was "a great book, full not only of learning, but of genius and stimulus." Even though Harnack possessed "powers and learning second to no man's of our generation," his defective presuppositions made him "one of the most destructive forces" in Christendom.[47]

Warfield's candid respect for radical critics reflects that he was sufficiently secure in his own position that he could admire the talents and self-confidence of his opponents without fear that such admission might be interpreted as a concession. Warfield believed his own position was unassailable despite his opponents' assaults upon it. His predecessors also were confident that their theology could withstand all attacks. In the 1820s Charles Hodge had fearlessly gone to Europe to prepare himself more adequately in biblical languages and criticism for his teaching responsibilities at the seminary. In his journal and his correspondence with Archibald Alexander, Hodge reveals challenges to his faith posed by exposure to Friedrich Schleiermacher's pantheism and his liberal synthesis of Christianity and romanticism. But despite the threats of new criticism and Schleiermacher's innovations, Hodge returned with his faith intact.[48] At the end of the century Warfield, firmly grounded in the same self-assured tradition, believed that he could successfully meet whatever Europe could send in written form to America.

During the last decade of the nineteenth century Warfield penned several articles surveying the current theological scene—its trends, recent developments, net gains and losses for conservatism. His most positive assessment of nineteenth-century scholarship was "The Century's Progress in Biblical Knowledge" (1900), while other articles such as "The Rights of Criticism and of the Church" (1892), "Evading the Supernatural" (1894), "Heresy and Concession" (1896), and "Recent Reconstructions of Theology" (1898) indicate by their titles the battles that the Princetonians were fighting.

Warfield was pleased that the century's scholars had greatly expanded the store of biblical knowledge. They had advanced the fruits of preceding centuries' biblical study to a greater degree of completion than had been accomplished in any previous era.[49] And as biblical knowledge grew, conservatives successfully blunted critical attacks. Although the century had been filled with controversy, he believed the Bible emerged "without so much as the smell of smoke upon its very garments."[50] While these remarks suggest that orthodoxy remained victorious in the academic arena, Warfield had to concede that his opponents' ranks had increased in number. In "Evading the Supernatural" he admitted that at the thought of Strauss's and Baur's popularity in Europe "American cheeks used to burn in indignation. But now [in 1894] "we have grown used to something like them at home."[51]

In order to appreciate why Warfield claimed victory despite the increasing number of opponents, we must examine the claims of radical critics as well as Warfield's response to them. Warfield's most lasting contribution to late nineteenth- and early twentieth-century scholarship was his analysis and criticism of its worldview. In responding to one theologian's statement that "theologies change as doth a garment," Warfield said this represents the contemporary "despair of dogmatics,"[52] which must have motivated him all the more to show the inadequacies of their presuppositions, methods, and conclusions. He disarmed the radical critics' claim that Christianity was merely another natural religion by demonstrating that such assertions arose not from an examination of the Bible itself, but from the naturalistic presuppositions that critics brought to their study of Scripture. Under such rubrics as "modernizing the faith" or "thinking through Christianity in modern terms" biblical critics and theologians justified refashioning Christianity to suit their own philosophies. Warfield's most telling rejoinder was that because demands for updating the faith are based on the obvious truth that every age "has a language of its own and can speak no other," too frequently critics invert the relation between Christianity and its contextual expression: "Instead of stating Christian belief in terms of modern thought, an effort is made, rather, to state modern thought in terms of Christian belief."[53] Warfield had occasion to use this criticism in the opening paragraphs of his reviews more than any other single point.

Typical of Warfield's approach is his review of Wilhelm Bousset's *What is Religion?* (1907). Warfield first establishes that Bousset is not simply an advocate of "comparative religion" nor of the "history of religion" but of the "comparative" or "history-of-religion [*Religionsgeschichte*] *school*" (my emphasis). Warfield's careful distinction alerts the reader that Bousset's method of studying religion was based on a carefully developed school of thought. His method was an outgrowth of an underlying philosophy or worldview that explains Christianity "in its entirety, as a religion among religions, the product like other religions of the religious nature of man." Warfield argues convincingly that Bousset adopts naturalistic assumptions "practically as a postulate" in his introduction.[54] By presupposing historical evolution, the author considered "impossible, . . . irreligious, and Godless" any claim that Old and New Testament religions are revealed and that all others are the product of human imagination.[55]

In the remainder of his review Warfield shows how at every point Bousset's interpretation of Christianity is a function of his philosophical perspective. Christianity is presented as a product of "the universal evolution of civilization," a development that began with animism and continued as a function of social organization through a series of increasingly complex stages until universal religions developed. Bousset claimed that Christianity emerged out of "the soil of its own time," and Jesus' singular innovation was his simplification of Judaism. But Jesus' religion was not Christianity's final form, because Christianity continued to evolve up to the modern period. Liberal scholars now jettison Paul's, Augustine's, and Luther's ideas of redemption, Christ's deity and atoning sacrifice, and a revealed Bible by contending they are not compatible with modern thought. Bousset finally reduces Christianity's content to the parable of the Lost Son, the forgiveness of sins, obedience to God's will, and eternal hope. Warfield pointedly remarks that whenever Christianity is "reduced to a 'natural religion' in its origin, it is reduced also to a 'natural religion' in its contents: it shrinks at once to the meager contents of the familiar trilogy, of God, morality, and immortality."[56]

In addition to exposing Bousset's worldview Warfield demonstrated that his "primal assumption" of naturalism was then buttressed by a biblical critical method involving another "immense assumption, or rather a whole series of immense assumptions" that included the Graf-Wellhausen critical reconstruction of Old Testament religion and history and the results of the "history-of-religions" reconstruction of New Testament religion. And behind these is the assumption of the traditional view's invalidity.[57] In the final analysis, Bousset's and other recastings of Christianity are merely a thoroughly consistent hypothetical construction: Bousset says, in effect, "See, if this be conceived to be the way religion has come into existence and developed itself in the course of the ages, then Christianity may be conceived to be a growth of nature. The 'if' here is, however, a mighty one. . . ." In Warfield's opinion, Bousset's radical criticism has no "argumentative value" whatsoever. He has not demonstrated that Christianity is what he claims it to be. Bousset has merely shown "that a self-consistent scheme of the origins of Christianity as a natural religion can be constructed."[58]

In a similar manner Warfield evaluated Dr. William Mackintosh's denial of miracles in *The Natural History of the Christian Religion*. Mackintosh's refutation appears to succeed only because a "more or less clearly formulated assumption of the impossibility of miracles underlies the strenuous opposition to the admission of their reality."[59] A direct outcome of the critics' claim that Christianity is a natural religion is their reinterpretation of its central doctrines beginning with biblical revelation. Warfield's most frequent assertion was that critical scholars were preoccupied with separating the "kernel from the husk." He charged that a scheme which presupposes that divine revelation in Scripture is separable from the "husk" of its historical expression inevitably led to the weakening of biblical authority. Warfield stressed two tendencies in liberal views of Scripture: critics redefine revelation and question the Bible's reliability.

Warfield's review of Reinhold Seeberg's *Revelation and Inspiration* (1909) begins with a reminder that Seeberg's goal is to "modernize" these doctrines. Warfield characteristically takes great pains to explain—several pages containing many citations from the text—Seeberg's view of *Heilsgeschichte*, God's redemptive history, narrated in Scripture. Significantly, Seeberg contended that even though Scripture is a record of God's redemptive history, the Bible is not always trustworthy in what it affirms. It includes some statements that are "notoriously false," outdated cosmologies, and errors in both worldview and interpretation of prophecy.[60] Yet in contrast to naturalists such as Mackintosh and Bousset, who contend that errors only confirm Scripture's natural origins, Seeberg attempts to salvage Scripture's value as a record of revelation despite its errors. His purpose, states Warfield, is "Pragmatistic" because the redemptive record's purpose in Scripture is to work in us "a remarkable inward experience, in which we find ourselves in the presence of God."[61] Warfield's assessment is very astute. Seeberg's introduction of a distinction between historical facts and ideas of revelation—the husk that is irrelevant and sometimes wrong and the kernel that produces our experience of redemption—substantially changes our conception of the Bible's authority.

> The basis of confidence is shifted from the Bible to Christian experience, or to what we used to call "the Christian consciousness," and the Bible is made to play the role only of vehicle of transmission. The whole conception of an authoritative book is set aside and we are to accept in the Bible only what Christian experience validates.[62]

Warfield terms Seeberg's interpretation an example of "Modern-positive Theology," which in his opinion is not really new. It is merely the latest expression of subjectivism, which can be traced back to Schleiermacher.

A final emphasis in Warfield's reviews was his criticism of liberal Christologies. His efforts not only to expose what he believed to be false christological thinking but also to articulate the Reformed viewpoint were untiring.[63] The Princeton apologist was especially skillful in confronting christological studies constructed on naturalistic premises. In 1911 he reviewed a series of Johannes Weiss's works on Christ. Warfield declared Weiss to be "[Wilhelm] Wrede's successor as the *enfant terrible* of the 'liberal school.' "[64] His opening remarks conform to his usual pattern of establishing that the author's worldview is the most significant factor shaping his Christology. Weiss's works, though destructive to the faith, have this "virtue," that they disclose in no uncertain terms "the violence of the assumptions on which alone the naturalization of the origins of the Christian religion can be accomplished."[65]

Weiss discusses the doctrine of Christ through the New Testament from the history-of-religions perspective. He admits that his view of Jesus is not the same as the New Testament's—that Jesus was a "resurrected and exalted Christ." Instead of what he called "primitive Christianity," Weiss espouses a theology that "has its full satisfaction in permitting itself to be led to the Father by Jesus of Nazareth."[66] Warfield explained that basic to liberals' distinguishing various views of Christ even within the New Testament was their tendency to reject Pauls' view, which Weiss called "not a development but a transmutation of the religion of Jesus."[67]

What astounded Warfield, however, is that Weiss, against all reasonable expectation considering his radical bias, refuses to take the liberal critical method to its absurd conclusion and join the most radical scholars who denied that Jesus even existed. Instead, Weiss assumes the improbable mantle of a conservative apologist by arguing in favor of the historical Jesus.[68] But he retains his mediating position between orthodox affirmations of Jesus' true historical existence only by abandoning his usual naturalistic critical method. Warfield revels in Weiss's being caught between two worldviews:

> Either he must continue to use the methods common to him and his more radical opponents, and then he can scarcely escape their extremities of negation. Or else he must allow the sounder methods he tells them they ought to follow, and then he can surely not fail ultimately to reach "conservative" conclusions. It appears to be only a new instance of the old difficulty: "I see the good; the evil I pursue."[69]

Warfield frequently mentioned Ernst Troeltsch's assertion that even though many scholars in Germany were turning to "reduced Christianity" advocated by the most radical critics, the radical school was manifesting no productive power in German culture and showed little future promise. Warfield took great comfort in Troeltsch's judgment that "almost all the religiousness of today draws its life from modifications of the strong religious treasures propagated in the churches and in them alone." Interestingly, Warfield's warmest endorsement of Troeltsch was that his usually consistent naturalism did not prevent him from affirming that Jesus' historicity was essential for Christianity. Warfield never tired of citing passage after passage in which Troeltsch either affirms the historical Jesus or rails against those who made Jesus merely a symbol expressing their peculiar faith in God.[70]

Our survey of Warfield's reviews demonstrates that although he never constructed his own systematic theology, conservatives ever since have been greatly in his debt. While some may argue that conservatives could have rallied around a fresh restatement of orthodoxy to stem the liberal tide, others could justly counter that Warfield discharged his stewardship in forms most suited both to his gifts and to current needs. Through his reviews, Warfield not only kept his followers abreast of liberal scholarship, but he also disarmed the critics by disclosing how dependent their ideas were on their naturalistic philosophy.

Of course, Warfield did more than analyze critical scholarship. He carefully honed an apologetic system by which he believed the conservative position could be defended. Having discussed his evaluation of naturalistic criticism, we now turn our attention to how Warfield showed that positive use of reason can establish Christian truth.

Common Sense Philosophy and Its Appropriateness to Reformed Theology

Warfield was convinced that simply because radical critics misused criticism, that fact certainly did not negate conservatives' responsibility to carry out its proper function. Contrary to widespread belief that conservatives oppose criticism, Warfield answered in "The Rights of Criticism and of the Church" (1892) that the existence of truth demands criticisms for its vindication. Biblical scholars are just as obligated to test the claims of the Bible as classical scholars are to examine Aristotle's works.[71]

Crucial to any critical scrutiny is establishing what Warfield called "the pure facts."

> Everyone of us exercises all the faculties God has given him and exhausts all the tests at his command to assure himself of the facts. . . . [Careful scrutiny of the facts] is good or bad in proportion to the accuracy and completeness with which the facts are apprehended and collected and the skill and soundness with which they are marshalled and their meaning read.[72]

A crisis has arisen, claims Warfield, not because of criticism itself but because of an "ineradicable tendency of man to confound the right of criticism with the rightness of his own criticism."[73] The Presbyterian Church must address modernism's proud claim to autonomy if it is to stand for the truth. Preserving revealed truth through apologetics has been vouchsafed to the church in the modern age just as it has been throughout history. Fundamental to Warfield's description of apologetics and his confidence that it would succeed in its task was his belief in Scottish Common Sense Philosophy (CSP). Philosophers in Scotland established commonsense principles in the eighteenth century to answer the skepticism of David Hume. Thomas Reid (1710-1796) argued that man's mind is so constituted by God as to know reality (not only the external world but also cause and effect and basic moral principles) directly by "common sense." John Witherspoon introduced Scottish philosophy in America when he became president of Princeton College in 1768. All the Princetonians learned it as the philosophical perspective by which they could not only achieve certainty in knowledge but also demonstrate fundamental apologetic truths. Princeton's dependence on this philosophy and particularly the question whether its use is consistent with Princeton's Reformed theology or whether it distorts their theology have stimulated heated debate between contemporary students and critics.[74] John Vander Stelt has written the most comprehensive, and critical, study of Scottish influence at Princeton in *Philosophy and Scripture: A Study of Old Princeton and Westminster Theology* (1978).[75] He explains how each of the Princeton thinkers was trained in Scottish philosophy and used its epistemological principles to ground his faith in rational certainty. Alexander used it to certify Scripture, Hodge developed it to construct an inductive method in theology, and Warfield carefully refined it into a rational apologetic system. Each development reflected the nature and intensity of opposition mounted against Princeton's position.

While he disagrees with all conservatives' use of Common Sense Philosophy, Vander Stelt is especially critical of Warfield's. Vander Stelt concedes that philosophical attacks increased after the Civil War and that Warfield believed that only a full-scale defense was capable of preserving Reformed thinking from crumbling. Nevertheless, he finds that Warfield's "entire framework of thought in his apologetics and Scripture is unmistakably intellectualistic" and has as its foundation a "dualism," an "ontological and religious distinction between the supernatural and the natural."[76] In one of his summary paragraphs on Warfield's thought, Vander Stelt explains this dualism:

> As to the structure of the natural world, Warfield found the basic assumptions of a philosophy of reality and truth that was greatly indebted to Scottish CSP acceptable and helpful in curtailing any threats upon certainty and security. By placing all of this within the larger context of the supernatural, Warfield tried to reinsure the former with the latter. Through a curious fusion of two basically conflicting worlds of thought, Warfield struggled to obtain theoretical and practical certainty for knowledge and faith by linking this certainty up with a *supra*-naturally qualified notion of infallibility and inerrancy that is supposed to be—but, in fact is not as the original autographs of the Bible are lost—within the reach of all rational men in this natural world.[77]

Thus Warfield took the Princeton faith in Common Sense to its furthest extreme without recognizing the vast internal tension it created within his system.[78]

In my previous work on Warfield I attempted to qualify some of the criticisms of Warfield's intellectualism and lack of emphasis on subjectivity that Vander Stelt has chosen to ignore.[79] While I agree with the central point of Warfield's critics, a defense can be made for his dependence on Common Sense principles. In a recent article Darryl Hart has defended Warfield's successor, J. Gresham Machen, on this point. His arguments apply with similar force to Warfield. Hart believes that Machen's continued adherence to Common Sense principles was a virtue despite its significant weaknesses. Without some of Common Sense Philosophy's principles epistemological skepticism might well have proven unavoidable. Its emphasis on universality, language, and history were not simply basic to knowledge but were also used in the defense of Christianity. All people are so constituted that they can know reality and communicate about it truthfully. Our knowledge of the past is something objective because memory is not just of an idea, but of the reality itself. These principles appeared fundamental as well to the biblical worldview, which holds man to be made in the image of God, recipient of a written revelation, and dependent on knowing certain objective redemptive historical events.[80] Long before Machen, Warfield used these principles repeatedly in his confrontations with liberal theology.

But an even more important factor in Warfield's retention of Scottish philosophy was his recognition of the bankruptcy in perspective of various philosophical systems that had replaced Common Sense. As we noted in the previous section, Warfield's skepticism of modern method was equally the match of modern thinkers' skepticism of traditional views of knowledge. Although he did not always refer to various philosophical systems, when he did, he barely concealed his contempt for them. Kantian epistemology, for example, in which the categories of the human mind take the place of God as the basis for knowing and in which God is reduced to a postulate of practical reason instead of its determining ground, represented "a veritable revolution by which God is dethroned and man elevated to His place as the center of the universe."[81] Kant's subjectivism was succeeded by Schleiermacher's, which ultimately gave way to Ritschlian thought. Frequently he attacked Albrecht Ritschl and his followers for their repudiation of metaphysics. Because the Ritschlites viewed revelation in purely personal terms and granted no place for propositions, they are unable to bequeath to the church anything more than "individualistic dogmatics."[82] In another summary for *The New York Observer* Warfield claimed that Ritschl's theology "was merely the old Socinianism in a new garment, cut from the cloth of Neo-Kantian speculation."[83] What Ritschl was attempting to do, Warfield continues, was to reduce Christianity's content to a nondogmatic faith. Thereby he hoped to save it from being ravaged by naturalistic philosophers, unbelieving scientists, and skeptical historians. While his motives may have been good, Ritschl made a common nineteenth-century error of gutting the Christian faith of its contents.[84]

Warfield's answer to modernist skepticism was that certainty is still achievable despite denials by contemporary philosophers and theologians. All that is required is a careful scrutiny of rational evidence. In an article written early in his career at Princeton, "Christian Evidences and Recent Criticism" (1888), Warfield claimed for rational apologetics virtually what he was to claim in 1900 about the Bible and criticism, that each had escaped from controversy without even the "smell of smoke" to suggest the battle. As we might expect, the method of proof for both was the same, examination of rational evidence—the facts.

Warfield's most memorable statement of Christianity's apologetic task was militant: "It is the distinction of Christianity that it has come into the world clothed with the mission to reason its way to dominion."[85]

The context of Warfield's remark is his rebuke of Abraham Kuyper's subordination of apologetics to the "narrow task of defending developed Christianity against philosophy, falsely so called."[86] One can sense Warfield's perplexity if not disdain as he claims that Kuyper's method of defending Christianity as only "the great assumption" bears all too much similarity to the hypothetical constructions of Bousset and Mackintosh. If Kuyper is correct, Christian scholars have been robbed of their incentives to validate Christian truth. The combined labors of exegetes, historians, and systematic theologians has "all hung, so to speak, in the air; not until all their labor is accomplished do they pause to wipe their streaming brows and ask whether they have been dealing with realities or perchance with fancies only."[87]

Several themes that we have examined so far coalesce in Warfield's repudiation of Kuyper's apologetics. Even more than he eschewed fancies in religious experience, Warfield despised them in theology and its preparatory discipline, apologetics. Conservatives, especially Reformed Christians in keeping with their holistic redemptive view, had a mandate not only to recapture Christian scholarship but also to regain the cultural mind.[88] These tasks in Warfield's opinion could never be accomplished by the Dutch apologetics of Kuyper and Bavinck. In his review of Bavinck's *De Zekerheid des Geloofs*, Warfield restates his commitment to evidentialist apologetics, which has the task among others of demonstrating God's existence and authenticating Scripture as God's Word. Christian faith, therefore, is a reasonable faith based on good and sufficient evidence, not a "blind and ungrounded faith."[89]

Warfield's frequent critique was that his opponents' theology was "Modern-Positive," as we saw above in his criticism of Seeburg. However, his own view of using "facts"—both rational facts to demonstrate God's existence and the authority of God's Word and biblical facts to arrive at a sound theology—sounds even more modern. His demand that critics ought to pay attention to facts carried the implication that liberals could be corrected if they would recognize the naturalism of their own position and scrutinize the evidence by virtually suspending their belief in naturalism just as phenomenologists advocate an epistemological epoche, "bracketing of existence," or suspension of belief in order to achieve greater accuracy in description of an object.[90]

Fortunately, in at least one significant writing, "The Right of Systematic Theology," Warfield discusses the influence of doctrine on facts. In the article Warfield challenged theologians and biblical scholars who were hostile to theology and saw in doctrine and propositional truth obstacles to religion. Some feared that doctrine would quench religious life and therefore they summarized Christianity as life, not doctrine. But the other group invented the watchword "Christianity consists of facts, not dogmas."[91]

Considering Warfield's predisposition to stress the objective or the factual basis of Christianity, we are not surprised that if given a choice between doctrine and facts, he would choose the facts. Nevertheless, consistent with many other instances in his writing he demands that neither can be relinquished; no antithesis is ever to be proposed which separates these two elements.

> What Christianity consists in is facts that are doctrines, and doctrines that are facts. Just because it is a true religion, which offers to man a real redemption that was really wrought out in history, its facts and doctrines entirely coalesce.[92]

All this we might have expected. But when Warfield discusses its implications he makes some strong statements that differ from his usually strict objective emphasis on facts.

> What is a fact that is wholly separated from what is here called "dogma"? If doctrines which stand entirely out of relation to facts are myths, lies [then] facts which have no connection with what we call doctrine could have no meaning to us whatsoever. It is what we call doctrine which gives all their significance to facts. A fact without doctrine is simply a fact not understood. That intellectual element brought by the mind to the contemplation of facts, which we call "doctrine," "theory," is the condition of any proper comprehension of facts.[93]

A few lines later, after quoting Dr. James Denney's statement that a fact without theory is a "blank unintelligibility, a rock in the sky, a mere irrelevance in the mind of man," Warfield adds that

> so closely welded are these intellectual elements—those elements of previous knowledge, or of knowledge derived from other sources —to facts as taken up into our minds in the complex act of apperception, that possibly we have ordinarily failed to separate them, and consequently, in our worship of what we call so fluently "the naked facts," have very little considered what a bare fact is, and what little meaning it could have for us.[94]

Certainly these few words do not make Warfield a presuppositionalist, just as Hart asserted that some of Machen's phrases did not make him one either. But Warfield never subjected facts to such searching criticism as he did in these words.

If the heirs of Warfield's evidentialist view and the advocates of Dr. Van Til's presuppositionalism are to make any progress in their internecine struggles, surely an item high on the agenda is a discussion of what constitutes a fact and how facts are to be used in both apologetic and theological disciplines. Was Warfield inconsistent in his apologetics, if only a few times? How are we to understand his use of Augustine's motto when we would have expected him to cite Thomas Aquinas' credo, "I understand in order that I might believe"? What is the significance of his basically presuppositionalist attack of his opponents in his reviews? What did he mean when he said that an "ineradicable tendency" in people makes them assert their own autonomy in critical studies? Has this any significance for discussions concerning the noetic effect of sin? How much effect, if any, do historical or contextual factors as well as individual subjective bias have on knowing, and can their effects be reduced or eliminated? Warfield's apologetic as a whole provides a vast storehouse of information for one side of the debate. But he was aware of other sides and established a precedent of interaction with them.

Conclusion

Benjamin B. Warfield's contributions to contemporary scholarship are more varied and complex than is immediately apparent. His scholarly production was voluminous and his range of interests spanned several theological disciplines. Even though his writing was often formal and his appeal was primarily to the scholarly community, he wrote on more than simply Reformed theology and the authority of Scripture where he left his considerable mark.

In the three areas that we have examined in this chapter we have noticed nuances and emphases that broaden our appreciation for Warfield's accomplishments. His piety was not exhausted by appeals to personal holiness and application of scriptural truth to one's private life. Even though his vision for a transformed American culture was cast in terms of his postmillennial faith, he challenges all followers of the Reformed tradition to rethink views of the visible church and of the leavening effect of the gospel in public life in order to extend what Warfield himself left unfinished.

Warfield's example in scholarly writing and particularly in the area of reviewing contemporary theology could hardly be more pertinent today. Reformed theologians need not only to continue to develop their theologies carefully in light of the Word of God but also to show how many contemporary theologians continue in the lines of their nineteenth-century counterparts by espousing twentieth-century presuppositions and proposals for action cloaked in terms borrowed from the Christian worldview.

Finally, Reformed theologians must continue to discuss how Christian truth can best be defended. The secularism that was building in

Warfield's day has become a dominant and established force at the end of the nineteenth century. Even though Warfield based his apologetic method on presuppositions that were more consistent with Scottish philosophy, he still possessed an essentially biblical vision of recapturing not only his church but also the wider culture with the gospel message.

Notes: Benjamin B. Warfield

1. Mark A. Noll, *Princeton Theology 1812-1921* (Grand Rapids: Baker Book House, 1983), 19.
2. A. A. Hodge, *Life of Charles Hodge* (New York: Charles Scribner's Sons, 1880), 382.
3. Ned B. Stonehouse, *J. Gresham Machen* (Grand Rapids: Wm. B. Eerdmans Publishing Company, 1954), 62.
4. Ibid., 63.
5. See Gary S. Smith, *The Seeds of Secularization* (Grand Rapids: Wm. B. Eerdmans Publishing Company, 1985), ch. 2.
6. Mark A. Noll, "The Founding of Princeton Seminary," *Westminster Theological Journal* 42 (1979): 72-110.
7. "The Relation between the Objective and Subjective Elements in Christian Religious Experience. A Study in the Systematic and Devotional Writings of Archibald Alexander, Charles Hodge, and Benjamin B. Warfield" (Ph.D. diss., Brown University, 1970) and *Piety and the Princeton Theologians* (Phillipsburg, NJ: Presbyterian and Reformed Publishing Company, 1981).
8. B. B. Warfield, "Authority, Intellect, Heart," in *Selected Shorter Writings of Benjamin B. Warfield,* ed. John E. Meeter, 2 vols. (Nutley, NJ: Presbyterian and Reformed Publishing Company, 1970), 1:668.
9. Ibid., 669.
10. Ibid.
11. Ibid., 670.
12. Ibid., 671.
13. "Spiritual Culture in the Theological Seminary," (1904), in ibid., 2:468-96 and "The Religious Life of Theological Students" (1911), in ibid., 1:411-22.
14. Ibid., 2:474.
15. Ibid., 412.
16. Ibid., 472.
17. He devoted more time to encouraging private piety, which he called "the center of our subject" (ibid., 481) and "the foundation stone of piety" (ibid., 1:422).
18. Ibid., 2:476.
19. Ibid., 477.
20. Ibid., 478.
21. Ibid., 1:418.
22. Ibid., 419.
23. In his excellent treatment of these issues Mark A. Noll probes Green's, Alexander's, and others' tendency to disparage active involvement in culture. They considered theological education to be the primary function of both the seminary and the college. Unfortunately, Princeton scholars were not devoted to

developing the Christian liberal arts. Noll also astutely argues that a symbiotic relationship should have existed between Princeton College and the seminary. The seminary should have provided the college "with the fruits of its labors from biblical study, theological reflection, and interaction with the Christian past," while on the other hand the college should have provided the seminary "with interpretations of modern learning and creative ventures of its own into the developing fields of nineteenth century thought." And both should have reflected "together on the foundational theological stances and philosophical presuppositions which shaped the inquiries of both bodies" (Noll, "Founding of Princeton Seminary," 105).

24. Hodge cited a list of corruptions in American society (divorce laws, desecration of the Sabbath, corrupt trade and commerce practices, and secularization of education) that needed to be redeemed by instituting Christian principles in public life. A series of impassioned questions revealed his concern over the dilution and elimination of Christian principles from American political, economic, and social institutions: "Whence come these portentous upheavals of the ancient primitive rock [Christianity] upon which society has always rested? Whence comes this socialistic earthquake, arraying capital and labor in irreconcilable conflict like oxygen and fire? Whence come these mad prehistoric anarchical ravings, the wild passages of a universal deluge which will blot out at once the family, the school, the church, the home, all civilization and religion in one sea of ruin?" (A. A. Hodge, *Popular Lectures on Theological Themes* [Philadelphia: Presbyterian Board of Publication and Sabbath School Work, 1887], 256).

25. Ibid., 334.

26. For a detailed view of the growth of secularization in American culture from the end of the Civil War to the beginning of World War I, see Smith, *Secularization*, ch. 2.

27. Warfield, *Shorter Writings*, 2:108.

28. Ibid., 108-09.

29. Ibid., 109.

30. Ibid., 110.

31. "John Calvin, the Man and His Word," in *Calvin and Calvinism* (New York: Oxford University Press, 1931), 20. In "Calvinism," an encyclopedia article originally written by Hodge but revised by Warfield, he narrates Calvin's effort to establish ecclesiastical freedom in Geneva. (See Warfield, *Shorter Writings*, 2:411.)

32. Warfield, *Shorter Writings*, 2:445.

33. Ibid., 184. He referred readers to Kuyper's Stone Lectures of 1898 at Princeton and to Emil Doumergue's "L'Art et le Sentiment dans l'oeuvre de Calvin" (1902) as correctives to the view that Calvin opposed artistic expression.

34. Ibid., 355.

35. "A Calm View of the Freedmen's Case," in ibid., 740. In words that might be labeled paternalistic today, Warfield calls on Christians to raise the blacks in their moral education. "The task before the American people in dealing with the blacks is nothing less . . . than the uprooting and expulsion of a settled and ingrained system of morality [which is the result of slavery itself] in order that a true morality may be substituted for it" (p. 737). Their social standing can only be compared to the caste system of India: "The harm that caste does toward those whom we would elevate cannot be overestimated. It kills hope; it paralyzes effort" (p. 741).

36. Ibid.

37. Ibid., 742.

38. Warfield quotes another commentator approvingly: "Emancipation has abolished only private but not public subjugation; has made the ex-slave not a free man but only a free Negro" (ibid., 744).

39. Ibid., 749.

40. Warfield's lack of comment on social issues is probably based on two factors: his temperament and his relatively secluded life. Unlike the Hodges who played significant roles in Presbyterianism, Warfield was confined to Princeton to care for his invalid wife. In his biography of Machen, Stonehouse said that Warfield rarely spent more than two hours away from her at a time and did not leave the town of Princeton between 1905 and 1915 (see Stonehouse, *Machen*, 220).

41. S. Ahlstrom, *A Religious History of the American People* (New Haven: Yale University Press, 1972). In each instance his discussion is inadequate considering Princeton's contribution to nineteenth- and twentieth-century theology and the depth of analysis Ahlstrom devoted to other movements such as Mormonism and Christian Science.

42. Ibid., 18. Winthrop Hudson in *Religion in America* (New York: Charles Scribner's Sons, 1965) discusses Warfield only briefly as a defender of the Westminster Confession and as instrumental with A. A. Hodge in forging the "Princeton doctrine of inspiration." Charles Hodge is discussed much more extensively. (Cf. pp. 167, 171, 180-81, 269, 284.)

43. For a cataloging of Warfield's articles and reviews see John E. Meeter and Roger Nicole, comps., *A Bibliography of Benjamin Breckinridge Warfield 1851-1921* (Nutley, NJ: Presbyterian and Reformed Publishing Company, 1974).

44. Cf. Patton's summary in his "Memorial Address," *Princeton Theological Review* 19 (1921): 387, explaining why Warfield never wrote his own systematics.

45. Due to limitations of space I will limit my remarks primarily to reviews collected in Vol. 10 of the Oxford series, *Critical Reviews* (New York: Oxford University Press, 1932), and to Warfield's *Shorter Writings*.

46. He credited Baur and his followers with pressing conservatives to increase their effort "to explore more deeply its record and to draw from them even more purely their treasures of truth" (Warfield, *Shorter Writings*, 2:9). In the very opening lines of one review of Ernst Troeltsch, Warfield said his "chief merit as a writer on theological themes lies in his straightforward downrightness" (*Critical Reviews*, 287).

47. Warfield, *Shorter Writings*, 2:451.

48. See my treatment of Hodge's trip in *Piety*, 48-52.

49. Throughout the article Warfield lists in detail major movements and publications in various areas of biblical scholarship, e.g., Old and New Testament, commentaries, textual aids, archeology, etc. Warfield was particularly gratified by exegetical gains.

50. Warfield, *Shorter Writings*, 2:13.

51. Ibid., 683.

52. *Critical Reviews*, 407.

53. Review of *Foundations. A Statement of Christian Belief in Terms of Modern Thought*, by Seven Oxford Men, *Critical Reviews*, 322.

54. *Critical Reviews*, 173.

55. Ibid.

56. Ibid., 177.

57. Ibid., 177-78.

58. Ibid., 178. I have included a detailed summary of Warfield's review of Bousset to indicate Warfield's careful and extensive treatment of the material and to show how radical Bousset's attack was.

59. "The Question of Miracles," in Warfield, *Shorter Writings*, 2:173. Later in the same essay Warfield evaluated David Hume's classic rebuttal of miracles. Hume's attack on the probability of miracles was based on the naturalistic assumption that our overwhelming experience of the uniformity of nature militates against their probability. But Hume's refutation is worthless as a rational argument. By affirming the absolute uniformity of nature, which renders miracles impossible, Hume is unable to answer the question of probability because probability "is the very thing in dispute" (p. 178).

60. *Critical Reviews*, 238.

61. *Critical Reviews*, 238.

62. *Critical Reviews*, 239.

63. Besides reviews, which are the focus of this paper, he produced numerous topical, exegetical, and historical studies. Cf. his *Christology and Criticism* (New York: Oxford University Press, 1929), and essays in *Shorter Writings*.

64. *Critical Reviews*, 266.

65. Ibid., 267.

66. Ibid., 286.

67. Ibid., 270.

68. Ibid., 273-74.

69. Ibid., 275.

70. Ibid., 294.

71. Warfield, *Shorter Writings*, 2:595.

72. Ibid., 596. Ascertaining the facts was as important in biblical study as it was in apologetics. In his review of Hastings' *Dictionary of the Bible*, Vol. 1, Warfield found it superior to other recently published works because of its greater reliability. But Warfield claimed that we still need a dictionary "which renounces speculation and sets out the facts" (*Critical Reviews*, 67). Warfield's remarks are reminiscent of Charles Hodge's statement on theological method in his *Systematic Theology*, that theologians use the facts of the Bible as a scientist uses the facts of nature. (See Vol. 1, pp. 1-17.)

73. Warfield, *Shorter Writings*, 2:596.

74. See Mark A. Noll's careful assessment of common sense as one of Princeton's "themes" in his excellent introductory chapter in *Princeton Theology*, 30-33, and George Marsden's assessments in *Fundamentalism and American Culture: The Shaping of Twentieth Century Evangelicalism, 1870-1925* (New York: Oxford University Press, 1980), 109-18.

75. Vander Stelt's notes and bibliography contain an extensive listing of scholarly works, including dissertations.

76. J. Vander Stelt, *Philosophy and Scripture: A Study of Old Princeton and Westminster Theology* (Marlburg, NJ: Mack Publishing Company, 1978), 182-83.

77. Ibid.

78. In the second part of his book Vander Stelt examines philosophy and Scripture at Westminster Seminary. He stresses the institutional shift away from Princeton Seminary led by Machen and the repudiation of Princeton's philosophical principles under Van Til's guidance. Perhaps Vander Stelt's sharp contrast between Princeton and Westminster might be seen as an attempt to win a hearing from Westminster for the Dutch tradition that he represents.

79. See Hoffecker, *Piety*, ch. 3. Vander Stelt refers to my work and uses some material on Hodge but does not concede that Warfield's work contained any subjective emphases.

80. D. Hart, "The Princeton Mind in the Modern World and the Common Sense of J. Gresham Machen," *Westminster Theological Journal* 45 (1984): 1-25. See also George Marsden's "J. Gresham Machen, History, and Truth," *Westminster Theological Journal* 42 (1979): 157-75.

81. *Critical Reviews*, 244.

82. *Critical Reviews*, 408.

83. Warfield, *Shorter Writings*, 2:449.

84. Ibid., 450.

85. Ibid., 99.

86. Ibid., 95.

87. Ibid., 96.

88. In "Christian Evidences and Recent Criticism" Warfield responded to Huxley's boast that "extinguished theologians lie about the cradle of every science as the strangled snakes beside that of Hercules." He retorted that "[theologians] keep company there with an interesting body of scientific lights"(!) (ibid., 129). Nevertheless, he continues, criticism such as Huxley's only spurs apologists to refine their arguments so that finally they may stand "easily victor against all modern assaults" (ibid., 131).

89. Ibid., 115. A rather significant historical irony is that while the Princetonians not only did not regain a hearing in American culture but also lost control of their Presbyterian denomination (see Lefferts Loetscher, *The Broadening Church* [Philadelphia: University of Pennsylvania Press, 1954]), the Dutch theologians continued to exercise significant cultural influence in their native Holland. See James Skillen and Stanley Carlson-Thies, "Religious and Political Development in Nineteenth Century Holland," *Publius* 12 (Summer 1982): 43-64.

90. Cf. "Phenomenology," in *Encyclopedia of Philosophy*, Vols. 5, 6 (New York: Macmillan Publishing Company, Inc., 1967), 140-44.

91. Warfield, *Shorter Writings*, 2:230.

92. Ibid., 234.

93. Ibid., 236.

94. Ibid.

4

J. GRESHAM MACHEN

W. STANFORD REID

J. Gresham Machen

J. Gresham Machen wielded a wide and important influence in his day, not only in Christian circles, but also on the entire American scene and beyond it. His fundamental motivation was his view of the Reformed theological position. He believed it was the most consistent and defensible expression of the Christian faith. A scholar, a leader, a powerful preacher, and at the same time a man of great charm, he was able to achieve much in his relatively short life. Caspar Wistar Hodge, who did not always agree with Machen, on hearing of his death stated that evangelical Christianity had lost its most outstanding leader and one of its greatest theologians. To understand Machen's importance on the American scene during the first third of this century we must understand his background, his theological development, and what he accomplished during his very active life.

Machen's Background and Development

In attempting to evaluate Machen's theological position and influence, we cannot avoid taking a quick glance at his background and development. But in so doing we have to keep in mind that the late nineteenth and early twentieth centuries were times of great upheaval in the Christian church, particularly in the Western world, with the rise of such phenomena as Higher Criticism, atheistic evolution, and the Marxist-socialist influences in government. The resulting conflicts in ecclesiastical circles in the Netherlands, the United Kingdom, and other countries spilled over into the American ecclesiastical situation with profound results. Consequently, to understand Machen's theological, apologetic, and social viewpoints we must look briefly at his personal experiences and background.

The home in which he was brought up was a Christian home, in which his ties with his mother were very close, and they remained so until the day of her death on October 13, 1931.[1] Educated first in a private school, he then attended Johns Hopkins University, from which he graduated in 1901 and went on to do a year's graduate work in classics under Basil L. Gildersleeve.[2] On his graduation he took his first of many trips to Europe, which whetted his appetite for further study in Germany. Before going to Europe for more academic work, however, he enrolled at Princeton Theological Seminary, although at this time he was by no means sure that he should enter the ministry. On the other hand, he seemed to feel that studying under such scholars as Francis Patton and Benjamin Breckinridge Warfield would be good training, no matter how he decided to spend his life.[3]

During his time at Princeton he had become very interested in the question of the virgin birth of Christ and had written a thesis on it, which was published in the *Princeton Theological Review* (1905-06). Even before this, however, he had left again for Europe to study at Marburg University, where he came under the influence of such Liberal theologians as Adolf Jülicher, Johannes Weiss, and Wilhelm Herrmann, all of whom caused him to have very serious doubts about the theological position that he had accepted at Princeton. From Marburg he went on to Göttingen where he studied under men such as W. Bousset who were as radically liberal as those at Marburg. Meanwhile some of his former professors had been pressing him to come back to Princeton to teach, an invitation that he finally accepted in 1906. He remained in the New Testament Department at Princeton until 1929.[4] But although he was an instructor in the seminary, he did not accept ordination until 1914. It took him eight years, with the help of W. P. Armstrong, Francis Patton, and others, to recover his faith after the experience in Germany.[5] In 1912 he really began his career as a writer with the publication of his address on "Christianity and Culture," and he followed that in 1915 with one on "History and Faith."[6] In both of these he laid down the foundation for most of his life's work, principles from which he never departed.

As he had gradually recovered his faith, Machen had become increasingly aware of the devastating effects of the Higher Criticism of the Scriptures and of the accompanying efforts to water down, if not to destroy entirely, its teachings.[7] As a result he felt convinced that the only answer to such attacks on the gospel was their refutation by an appeal to the historical sources and a proper "common sense" interpretation of their statements. The outcome of this conviction was a number of addresses dealing with such topics as the virgin birth and the resurrection of Christ, which were later published. In these he took a very definite stand on the historical reliability of the biblical record, and devoted considerable time to criticizing and refuting the modernist position. This, however, brought him into conflict with some of the seminary

authorities. Although in 1926 the Directors wanted him to become professor of apologetics, a move to which he was not much inclined, the
Trustees, led by the president, J. Ross Stevenson, were opposed. The
result was a battle that led to the reorganization of the administration:
the Board of Directors was abolished and full control of the school was
given to a single Board of Trustees to which two signers of the liberal
Auburn Affirmation were appointed. The resulting conflict between
Machen and the new administration led to his resignation from the seminary in June 1929, on the ground that Princeton had now left its historic
theological position.[8]

With the departure of Machen, some others connected with the
seminary felt they too should go. As a result they formed a committee
to establish a new seminary, Westminster, which opened in Philadelphia
as an independent educational institution in the autumn of 1929. In
his address at the opening of the new institution, Machen stressed two
articles of its constitution. One was the final authority of the Bible, which
he characterized as "a plain book addressed to plain men, and . . . it
means exactly what it says." The other was that since Princeton was now
"lost to the evangelical cause," the new seminary would stand firmly for
the Reformed theological position as expressed in the Westminster
Confession of Faith. Added to that, he warned that anyone coming to
Westminster would find that being a student would entail hard work![9]
Naturally Princeton was not pleased with this development, and when,
a few years later, the present writer visited Princeton to see some friends,
he was given a detailed diagnosis of "Dossie's" paranoia.

The establishment of Westminster, however, did not bring Machen
peace and ease of mind. He was also faced with the problem of what
would happen to the graduates of the seminary when they were prepared
to seek ordination. Some might, of course, go to denominations other
than the Presbyterian Church, U.S.A., but he was most anxious that
they should enter his church in the hopes of bringing about a true reformation. About this time the novelist Pearl Buck, serving as a missionary in China for the Presbyterian Church's Board of Missions, published
in *The Christian Century* an enthusiastic review of the radically liberal
Rethinking Missions, and followed that in January 1933 with an article in
Harper's Magazine on the propriety of Christian missions, in which she
virtually ruled out the New Testament message as a mystical concept of
Christianity, rejecting even the need for the historic person of Christ.
When the Board of Missions, while continuing to support Buck, then
turned down a Westminster graduate who applied for appointment, and
the General Assembly followed this with a vote of confidence for the
board, Machen and others felt that action had to be taken. The result
was the formation of the Independent Board for Presbyterian Foreign

Missions.[10] Against this move the Presbyterian Church took vigorous action, ordering that the Independent Board be dissolved. When that was not done, the judicial commission took action to discipline the participants, who either resigned or were defrocked. Among them was Machen.[11] Following this the only answer was the formation of a new Presbyterian church. The Presbyterian Church of America, later the Orthodox Presbyterian Church, was organized in 1936.[12]

Yet even the formation of a new church did not solve all problems. For one thing, some of Machen's supporters in the formation of Westminster Seminary, such as Professor Oswald T. Allis and Clarence Macartney, had not favored the formation of the Independent Board, and when plans were laid for the organization of a new Presbyterian church, they withdrew entirely along with some others. This was a great disappointment to Machen. But even more of a blow came when Carl McIntire and J. O. Buswell withdrew to form the Bible Presbyterian Church because of the new church's refusal, under Machen's guidance, to alter the Westminster Confession to make it more premillennial and to require total abstinence from alcoholic liquors a condition of church membership.[13] Added to all this the members of the Independent Board were now divided, for some were not particularly interested in establishing a new Presbyterian church, but instead favored independency.

At this point Machen was invited to go out to North Dakota for the Christmas holiday, which he did, but sadly while traveling around the state in the intense cold he contracted pneumonia and on January 1, 1937, died.[14] So ended the career of one of America's great defenders of the faith.

Machen's Theology

Machen's methodology is basic to an understanding of both his theology and his defense of it. He was not primarily a philosopher, which explains his reluctance to move from the New Testament department to become professor of apologetics at Princeton, and also his enthusiasm for the appointment of Cornelius Van Til to that position. Nor was he primarily a systematic theologian, although he knew his Reformed theology and was prepared to expound it whenever possible, as we can see from his *What Is Faith?* and the two volumes of his radio addresses delivered just before his death.[15] Unfortunately he died before he could complete the radio series, but despite this misfortune, he clearly indicates his grasp of the system of Reformed theology. The fact is that he was a historian, as he indicated in the opening sentence of his 1915 essay "History and Faith" which stated that "the student of the New

Testament should be primarily an historian. The centre and core of all the Bible is history."[16]

Because of this historical orientation, he sought to prove the reliability of the biblical record by a sound historical investigation and analysis of the evidence provided by the documents. One only has to note the course he established on the introduction to the literature and history of the New Testament to realize this. Or what was even better, if one could attend his lectures on Apostolic History and listen to his enthusiastic presentation of the evidence for single authorship of the Gospel of Luke and the Acts of the Apostles, one would soon realize that he was indeed a sound and well-trained historian. His constant insistence in both his expository and his apologetic works on the validity of his historico-grammatical exegesis of the Bible was further evidence of his point of view. Some, even of his followers, however, have claimed that he followed too completely the Scottish Common Sense Philosophy of Thomas Reid, failing to take into consideration the question of the presuppositions of one's thinking. For this some have even declared him merely nineteenth century in his approach. It must be constantly kept in mind, however, that while he insisted that the validity of the historical analysis could lead one to accept facts as true, it did not then lead automatically to acceptance of the doctrine behind those facts. As he pointed out more than once, while one might acknowledge that history showed that Christ died, more was required for one to confess that he died for our sins. He could even state that a non-Christian might believe in Christ's resurrection, but it was only by the work of the Holy Spirit that that individual would believe that Christ rose victor over death for the sinner's justification. The presuppositions or faith of the Christian led to a very different understanding from that of the unbeliever, who began with very different presuppositions.[17]

As mentioned earlier, Machen had come to this specifically Reformed position only gradually. His home background seems to have been evangelical, but not strongly Reformed. During his time of study in Germany he undoubtedly had faced a large number of problems, particularly in dealing with the attacks of the various theological professors on the historical reliability of the New Testament, and had eventually come to realize that without the basic Christian faith, even historical evidence would not bring conviction of the truth of Christianity. This comes out very clearly in his lectures at the Grove City Bible School in 1925, which later appeared as the volume *What Is Faith?* and his radio addresses over station WIP, Philadelphia, just shortly before his death. True, he did not work out the whole problem of presuppositions as did Cornelius Van Til, but he certainly never ignored them in favor of a positivistic view that held that the facts were all that were needed.

Because of his own presuppositions he followed the Reformed position that the Bible is the Word of God. But by doing so, he did not accept a mechanical type of dictation. He held the view that the writers of the Bible used the ordinary sources of information, that they as individuals had personal freedom but that they recorded the facts and their interpretation guided by the Holy Spirit, so that the Bible is truly infallible, the Word of God in the word of man.[18] Hence in order to gain a true and proper understanding of the divine revelation one must study the Bible by the grammatico-historical method. The trouble with so many of the so-called Liberals, he maintained, was that they refused to employ the proper historical method honestly and so twisted the meaning of the Scriptures.[19] A true evangelical and Reformed exegesis, on the other hand, employed the scientific historical method that is the true foundation and source of a sound Christian theology.

When one turns to a study of Machen's actual theology, one finds at its core a typically Reformed doctrine of God. God is triune: Father, Son, and Holy Spirit. This God is sovereign, a theme of which he never became tired. As one reads his various works, whether those primarily expository or primarily apologetic, the sovereignty of God is a constantly recurring note. But equally important in his thought was the fact that God is a gracious and loving God. As he pointed out in the second chapter of *What Is Faith?*, we can believe in God only as we know him, and this means that we must know him as he reveals himself to us in nature, in our own souls, and in the Scriptures of the Old and New Testaments. When we so know him we believe in him and trust ourselves to his sovereign grace.[20]

Only, however, as one comes to God through Jesus Christ, the incarnate Savior, does one truly know God. And Machen, as a New Testament scholar, was therefore very interested in setting forth evidence and arguments for the reliability of the New Testament's witness to Christ as the incarnate divine Savior. His first major work dealing with this matter appeared in 1921 under the title *The Origin of Paul's Religion*. In 1925 and 1926 he had two articles published on the virgin birth and resurrection of Christ, and another in the following year dealing directly with the apostolic witness to Christ.[21] But probably his most important work in this field was *The Virgin Birth of Christ*, published in 1930. In all of these writings he constantly insisted that the different writers of the New Testament books were united in their testimony to Christ.

This testimory was that he is the Son of God, the Savior of the world. In this testimony there was first the fact that he was conceived miraculously in the womb of Mary and thus was the son of a virgin. Machen also spends considerable time with Christ's divine powers and works. These he cites as witnesses to the fact that he was not merely a great and good mortal, but both God and man in one person. At the same time, Machen stresses Christ's teachings as being very relevant and applicable not only to the church, but also to society in our own day and age. Yet he was not prepared to accept the view that Christ's teachings were merely the setting forth of a moral code. They were far different, for Christ said very clearly and certainly that he was much more than merely a teacher. He was the Savior, the promised Messiah.

This stress on Christ as Savior was the expression of Machen's basic religious faith. Rejecting the view that he was merely a teacher and an example, Machen insisted that it is only as one places one's trust in Christ as his Savior who died on Calvary's cross and who rose the third day and ascended into heaven, that one may obtain the forgiveness of sins. Only then may one be truly called a Christian. In his chapter "Faith in Christ" in *What is Faith?* he constantly attacks and criticizes those who would dilute the New Testament message that Christ is the only Savior of men. And if one listened to his preaching one would very quickly realize that the preacher was in every respect an evangelist as well as a scholar. Machen's wholehearted conviction that Christ was *his* Savior is illustrated by his sending a telegram, one of the last acts before his death, to Professor John Murray, in which he said: "I'm so thankful for the active obedience of Christ. No hope without it."[22]

While Machen did not stress the work of the Holy Spirit as he did that of Christ, nevertheless the presence, power, and work of the Third Person of the Trinity is always taken into account when discussing the works of God. One only has to glance at the subject indices in his various works to see this statement borne out. Although he did not lay great stress upon it, Machen accepted the doctrine of Common Grace as part of the work of the Spirit. But even more important was his constant emphasis upon the work of the Spirit in the incarnation, in the writing of the biblical books, and in the regeneration and sanctification of the elect. In this he was following closely in the footsteps of Calvin. The application of Christ's saving work is the action of the Spirit, who in doing this bears witness to both the Father and the Son. In fact, that witness-bearing is what results in both regeneration and faith.[23]

Basic, however, to Machen's view of divine redemption was his insistence upon the doctrines of creation and providence. He emphasized the necessity of realizing that the triune God had created all things out of nothing and constantly sustained and ruled over them from moment to moment. He rejected all deistic or pantheistic attempts either to separate God from creation or to make him simply the essence of creation itself. And he insisted upon the necessity of recognizing the divine creatorship, because nature was the primary means of divine revelation since it was the "work of God's hand." Hence his great appreciation of the beauties of mountain climbing and natural scenery. But especially important was the necessity of recognizing that the creation of man was central to creation, and it was in creation that the drama of God's redemptive work was enacted.[24]

Machen's stress upon the saving work of Christ and the regenerating and sanctifying work of the Spirit arises out of his acceptance of what the Bible says about man. He accepted the doctrine of the Fall without any question, for he could see the sinfulness of man all around, and within. His introduction to *What is Faith?* as well as the chapter "Faith Born of Need" makes this only too clear. Because of man's sin he is alienated from God and has no desire to be reconciled to God, unless God takes the first step and draws the sinner to himself. This reconciliation is the only way in which man may inherit eternal life. Twelve years after he had stated the Reformed position in *What is Faith?* he dealt in his last radio addresses (published after his death under the title *The Christian View of Man*) with the subjects of the creation of man, the covenant of life, man's fall, and God's gift of grace. There he rings the changes on man's sinfulness, but also on God's sovereign predestination, and his working out of that predestination in history.

It is to be regretted that Machen did not live to present the third of his series of radio talks, which would have dealt with the subject of salvation. But the Lord saw fit to take him before that could happen. From his other writings, however, one can understand quite clearly that what he would have said would have been quite in accord with the Reformed tadition. One could quote many passages from his various writings, but perhaps one from *What is Faith?* brings out his views most clearly.

> Certainly, at bottom, faith is in one sense a very simple thing; it simply means that abandoning the vain effort of earning one's way into God's presence we accept the gift of salvation which Christ offers so full and free. Such is the "doctrine"—let us not be afraid of the word—such is the "doctrine" of justification through faith alone.[25]

"Justification by faith alone"—the words of Martin Luther, John Calvin, and the other Protestant Reformers looking back to the Apostle Paul and to Jesus Christ himself—was central to Machen's own Christian experience and so to his thought. Moreover, he knew that this faith was the gift of God through regeneration by the Holy Spirit.[26]

Faith, however, meant loving obedience. He did not hold, as do some modern theologians who claim to be Reformed, that obedience is part of faith, that one is justified by "obedient faith."[27] Works are the outgrowth, the result of faith, not part of it. This he reiterated repeatedly in his chapter "Faith and Works" in *What is Faith?* That one had faith in Christ as Savior resulted in a love for him and obedience to him. This means that the Christian is to obey Christ in all things, even in the ministry of the church. As he put it in a graduation address to the students of Westminster Seminary in 1934, in the midst of the conflict over the Independent Board:

> If you obtain your message from any other authority than the Word of God, if you obtain it from the pronouncements of presbyteries or General Assemblies, then you may wear the garb of ministers, but you are not ministers in the sight of God. You are disloyal to the Lord Jesus Christ: you have betrayed a precious trust. [28]

From this statement we can see that for Machen the central directory of the Christian life was the Scriptures, enlightened by the Holy Spirit in the hearts and minds of faithful Christians. [29]

Unfortunately Machen did not have much to say about eschatology. "Unfortunately" because a thorough study of New Testament teaching on this subject might have helped quite a number of people who were led to reject him as a teacher and a leader because he was not a premillennialist. That he held the amillennial position he stated on a few occasions. Furthermore, when an attempt was made in the early days of the Presbyterian Church of America to change the Westminster Confession to allow more room for premillennialism, he opposed it. He held strongly, however, to the view that God ruled over history and was leading it on to the consummation of all things. More important, apparently, in his thinking was the Christian hope of eternal life in the presence of God, where all things would be made new. [30] Again turning to *What is Faith?* this comes out very clearly in the last chapter "Faith and Hope." No doubt if he had lived to complete his series of radio addresses he would have dealt with this topic in more detail. [31]

In summing up Machen's theology one can only say that it was the theology of a typically Reformed scholar. He did not produce a systematic theology in the usual form, but sought to present doctrine in a popular manner that the ordinary layperson could understand. As he remarked when criticizing A. C. McGiffert's work *The God of the Early Christians,* although he did not agree with it, "it possesses at least one merit that is rare among contemporary religious literature—it is interesting." [32] Machen sought to write books with a similar popular appeal. At the same time, he was always ready to defend the faith, with the result that much of his work was taken up with apologetics. To this we now turn.

The Defense of the Faith

Although Machen's primary interest was the exposition of Christian doctrine, a very close second was his view that the Christian faith must be set forth as a valid system of thought. He believed that a radical change was needed in both the church and society in general. This would come only if there were a reformation similar to that which took place in the sixteenth century, and it would take place only if Christians were prepared to stand up and present the credentials of their beliefs, showing that they met all the requirements of sound thinking. While he acknowledged that ultimately man could not penetrate the mystery of God and the divine purpose or counsel, yet there was enough evidence in the Scriptures to show that what they said was true and historically verifiable.[33]

He felt the need for apologetics centered around the message of the gospel as set forth primarily in the four Gospels and in the writings of the Apostle Paul. Wherever he turned there seemed to be theologians, preachers, journalists, and others who were prepared to attack the Christian's faith and demonstrate that it had been misinterpreted or twisted to be something that was radically different from the historic doctrines. There were those in his own church, such as the signers of the Auburn Affirmation, who while not rejecting Christianity, at least officially, so undermined all basic doctrine that nothing was left. At the same time there were those who simply rejected the Christian teachings as completely wrong. In this class were people such as H. L. Mencken, Pearl Buck, and Albert C. Dieffenbach, who, while acknowledging Machen's strength of character and his loyalty to his position, yet rejected his ideas out of hand.[34]

In the face of dilutions of and direct attacks on the historic Reformed position Machen sought to put up a strong and effective defense. To do this, he insisted that it was possible to prove that the books of the New Testament were historically trustworthy. He maintained that the grammatico-historical approach to and interpretation of the documents, used with "common sense," would show that what they said was true. In this he was clearly following the line of thought of the Princeton school of apologetics, which in turn looked back to Thomas Reid's Scottish "Common Sense Philosophy." And whenever he had the opportunity he went after the Modernists who were attempting to undermine the Christian faith with their twisted and perverted interpretations. His first extensive work in this area was *Christianity and Liberalism*, first published by Macmillan in 1923, but republished seven times, the last printing being done in 1940, three years after his death.

Machen, however, did not believe that merely historical or rational arguments would convince an unbeliever and bring him to faith in Christ. As he pointed out more than once, while a person might know all the arguments for Christ's virgin birth or his resurrection, that person would come to faith only through the action of the Holy Spirit in regenerating the individual. Being very conscious of the noetic influence of sin, which effectively blocked man's spiritual vision, and also of the perversion of the human will, he recognized that even true "common sense" would ultimately make no sense to an individual unless the Holy Spirit opened that person's eyes and changed his or her will. Only then would the person believe.[35]

Having to depend upon the Holy Spirit to bring conviction to the unbeliever did not mean that Machen held to a kind of quietist position in which he waited passively until the Spirit moved. He maintained that the Christian, particularly the preacher, had the duty of proclaiming the gospel wherever and whenever he had the opportunity. Thus he was always ready to present his theological position and defend it even before quite skeptical audiences or in the secular press such as *The New York Times*, *Forum*, and *The Annals* of the American Academy of Political and Social Science. He did not doubt that he could prove his case if his critics and opponents would only stick to the facts and not attempt to circumvent them by irrational theories.[36] All this meant that the Christian must have freedom to proclaim the gospel and in so doing to evangelize. The gospel had to be carried to the far corners of the earth and it was not to be merely a gospel of feeling or sentiment, but was to have a sound intellectual basis, founded firmly on the revelation contained in the Scriptures.[37]

To carry out what he considered his God-given mandate to stand for the truth of the gospel necessarily involved Machen in controversy, particularly within the Presbyterian Church, U.S.A. He believed that it was the duty of all orthodox Christians to take their stand within the church against those who would pervert the gospel, thus depriving people of the knowledge of God's grace. He also felt that those who had signed the Westminster Confession and then proceeded to undermine its teachings by preaching and teaching doctrines and theories that were in conflict with it were dishonest and should be exposed for what they actually were doing. Since much of the administration of both Princeton Seminary and of the church as a whole seemed to be in the hands of such individuals, Machen was prepared to speak out no matter how unpopular such action would be, and he was maligned for so doing. He refused to modify his position, however, or give in to pressure.[38]

Machen, however, was no schismatic or secessionist. He did not follow the example of so many Christians who refuse "to get involved," and simply withdraw. He stayed in and fought until forced out. He left Princeton because he felt that the entire institution had given up its basic Reformed position, and helped to found Westminster to carry on the Princeton tradition.[39] But he did not leave the Presbyterian Church. Nor did he leave the church later when he helped to organize the Independent

Board, since the official board was accepting candidates who rejected the church's accepted doctrinal standards. Rather, he felt it necessary to organize a board that would maintain the church's professed theological position. The present writer can well remember a speech he made on "set-up" night to the Westminster Dining Club in 1936. After outlining the situation in the Presbyterian Church, U.S.A. at the time, he said forcefully: "But boys, I am not going to leave. This is my church, and I am staying in and fighting until they either change the Confession or throw me out." And they did the latter.[40]

Thus one may see that Machen's apologetic approach was no merely theoretical, classroom stance. It was a desire to defend and maintain the heart of the gospel. As he put it in his essay "Christianity and Liberty":

> Increasingly the great alternative is becoming clearer; give Jesus up, and confess that His portrait is forever hidden in the mists of legend; or else accept Him as a supernatural Person, as He is presented by all the four Gospels and by Paul.[41]

This was his position, and for it he was prepared to do battle both in the church courts and in the world at large.

The Application of the Faith

As we have endeavored to show, Machen was no ivory-tower scholar. One indication of this is his intense interest in the fortunes of the football teams of the area, and he frequently took interested students to see the Army-Navy game, which seems to have been his favorite sports spectacle. Also contrary to much popular opinion, especially at Princeton, he had a strong sense of humor. One who has attended his classes can vouch for that, for his humor appeared even in his lectures. But even more important was his insistence that a good minister must be a stunt man. As a result there was an annual Westminster stunt night at which he was frequently the star as he recited poetry satirizing the weaknesses and foibles of human nature. He was anything but the paranoid individual that many of his foes insisted upon picturing.

In the social field, Machen's primary interest was in the maintenance of freedom for the individual. He was strongly opposed to the increasing tendency toward collectivism in society that he saw growing on every hand. He felt that the civil government was forever attempting to regulate and control in order to make all citizens of the same pattern and so destroy the individual's wish to be an individual, different from others. He himself was no conformist, and he did not feel that others should be made to conform to the humors of a group of bureaucrats in Washington or in one of the state capitols. Therefore, he was constantly, and on every appropriate occasion, demanding that the individual should have liberty consonant with the liberty of his fellow citizens. Where true Christianity reigns, liberty is the rule. "God is free, and where He is, there is liberty and life."[42]

Some of his opponents objected to his call for liberty at the same time that he demanded the disciplining of heretics within the church. Where was the freedom for which he fought? He pointed out, however, that there is a difference between voluntary and involuntary organizations. The state is an involuntary organization of which one is a member whether he wishes or not. The state that interferes with one's liberty must be restrained. In the case of a voluntary organization such as the church, no one is forced to enter. "Insistence on fundamental agreement within a voluntary organization is therefore not at all inconsistent with insistence upon the widest tolerance in the state."[43] He consequently insisted that the church not only had the right but also the duty to remove those who contravened the fundamental agreement. Thus he was prepared to battle for wide freedom under the state, but at the same time for close adherence to the constitution of voluntary bodies such as the church.

Machen's concept of state tolerance was not just centered on one or two things, but seems to have had a wide-angle lens. For instance, the story went the rounds at Westminster Seminary that at one point the city council of Philadelphia proposed enacting a law that would have forbidden jaywalking. An open session of the council was held to determine whether the people of the city wanted such a rule. Machen, who appeared at the council, voiced strong opposition to the rule as an infringement of the citizens' freedom and was to a considerable extent responsible for the proposal being dropped. Although he did not live to see it, he pointed out that the constant eroding of freedom would lead to national and international disasters throughout the world. He should have lived to 1984!

Liberty of action generally, however, was not the only aspect of Machen's concern. He was particularly interested in the matter of freedom of choice in education and backed the concept of the Christian school. He viewed the education of his own day as falling far short of what true education should be, pointing out that there was a tendency toward theory and not an emphasis upon learning the facts. He stressed the view that merely learning some techniques or methods of approaching facts was not really education. He felt that the whole idea of learning as a discipline involving the entire individual was being disregarded. In addition he insisted that while technical education was important, the study of broader subjects such as the humanities was being neglected, as were all attempts at moral education. "By this purely secular, non-moral and non-religious, training we produce not a real human being but a horrible Frankenstein. . . ." Furthermore, such education seeks to make everyone conform to one pattern or mold and teaches that all religious faiths are of the same value and that character must be built upon human experience, rather than upon the law of God.[44] It was these latter considerations that weighed so heavily in his mind in his opposition to the whole system of compulsory public education. But he also opposed any attempt to introduce Bible reading into the public schools, since that, too, could be dangerous, for without proper direction the Bible message could be distorted and changed. Furthermore, it would conflict with the whole concept of freedom of religion.[45]

The solution to this problem, as far as Machen was concerned, was the Christian school. True, he recognized that not every place had or could afford such a school. If that were the case, then there should be released-time instruction. If on the other hand it would be possible to have a Christian school that could teach from a truly Christian perspective, such a school should be established. However, and this was important to his thought, the parents must be able to determine. He pointed out that certain laws that had been proposed in Congress aimed at taking away the parents' right to determine their children's training, placing it instead in the hands of governmental bureaucrats. This he felt was definitely wrong and should be stopped.

The reason for Machen's preference for the Christian school was twofold. In the first place he believed that released time tended to give schoolchildren the idea that Christianity affected only a part of life, and a not very significant one at that. Most of life was dealt with in the secular-humanistic classrooms of the public school. Second, insisting that Christianity gave a world-and-life view that dealt with all aspects of human existence, he held that the entire curriculum of the Christian school should be taught from that point of view. At the same time, he stressed that the Christian school must do its job effectively so that even those who were not Christians would give it their backing, not only for its teaching but because "they really love freedom and the noble traditions of our people." Even more important was the need for the Christian part of the nation to give its support to the Christian school, not as a competitor of the Christian family, but as a support to what Christian parents were seeking to do in the home.[46]

Although Machen made no claim to be a prophet, nor the son of a prophet, many of the questions that he raised with regard not only to education, but to the whole structure of the Anglo-American cultural patterns seem to be moving toward a fulfillment that he foresaw. He was strongly opposed to the establishment of a federal Department of Education that would so regulate education that everything in that field would become monolithic and at the same time, in order to accommodate everybody, would maintain minimum standards. We are now beginning to see this in innovations such as "Process Writing," which are being introduced into schools, with the result that many college freshmen now have to take remedial English courses in order to be able to do their academic work. And much the same effect may be seen in other fields, even in automobile manufacture where thousands of cars have to be recalled each year in order to remedy mechanical defects of one kind or another. To Machen this would not be in any way surprising.[47]

The only solution to this problem would be a new Reformation. This would not be a harking back to the sixteenth century, but a new Reformation wrought by the Spirit of God in the contemporary Christian church. The result would be a restoration of true liberty to mankind in which "thinking [would] again come to its rights." Theological Modernism, which has led to much of the intellectual degradation of the day, would be pushed aside by those who were characterized by faith in Christ as Savior and Lord, and who, possessed "by an heroic honesty," would take their stand without any consideration of consequences. With such a movement, he believed, would come a new Renaissance that would encourage true originality, independence of mind, and "plain common sense."[48]

Such was the theological position of J. Gresham Machen and his application of it. Theologically he was not significantly different from his teacher B. B. Warfield, nor from John Calvin, nor even from the writers of the New Testament. His, however, was a different situation and set of circumstances from theirs. Faced with a decline in Reformed orthodoxy at Princeton and in the Presbyterian Church, U.S.A., and with the growing influence of godless, materialistic humanism in society as a whole, he was prepared to speak out. Believing in the objectivity of truth and employing a sound critical-historical approach to the Christian faith as set forth in the Bible, the Word of God, he attacked the growth of heresy within the Presbyterian Church, and also sought in very practical ways to offset and circumvent the forces that he believed were carrying it in a direction that would destroy it as a true Christian church. At the same time, he took his stand against the humanistic trends in society, calling for Christians to assert themselves as members of society, in order that they might be salt that has not lost its savor. He hoped and prayed for a new Reformation that would revive the church, and renew and reform the social structures.

In the introduction to this volume, George Marsden has delineated three types of Reformed theology: the doctrinal, the cultural, and the evangelistic. In a very real sense, Machen embraced all three. He represented the first in his strong defense of the doctrines of the faith; the second in his constant emphasis upon the Christian's responsibility to take social action; and the third in his willingness to proclaim the grace of God in Jesus Christ whenever he had an opportunity. For these reasons his influence went far beyond the confines of the Reformed community in America.

But how much influence did he have? This, of course, is hard to estimate. Undoubtedly he influenced many of his students at both Princeton and Westminster, but his sudden decease at a relatively early age appears to have cut back this influence, at least in the eyes of those who see such events only in their space-time context. It may well be, however, that in the purpose and plan of God he succeeded in sowing seed that may be part of the spiritual harvest that will bring to fruition the Reformation for which he longed.

Notes: J. Gresham Machen

1. Ned B. Stonehouse, *J. Gresham Machen: A Biographical Memoir* (Grand Rapids: Wm. B. Eerdmans Publishing Company, 1954), 564.

2. Ibid., 42, 47ff.

3. Ibid., ch. 3.

4. Ibid., chs. 5-6.

5. Ibid., 193ff.

6. Ibid., 205-06; J. G. Machen, *What Is Christianity? and Other Addresses*, ed. Ned B. Stonehouse (Grand Rapids: Wm. B. Eerdmans Publishing Company, 1951), 156-85.

7. D. G. Hart, "The Princeton Mind in the Modern World and the Common Sense of J. Gresham Machen," *Westminster Theological Journal* 45 (1984): 10ff.

8. Stonehouse, *J. Gresham Machen*, 441ff.

9. Machen, "Westminster Seminary: Its Plan and Purpose," in *What Is Christianity?* 224ff.

10. Cf. Machen, "The Christian View of Missions," in *What Is Christianity?* 148ff.; Stonehouse, *J. Gresham Machen*, 472ff.

11. Ibid., 491.

12. Ibid., 495ff.

13. Ibid., 504.

14. Ibid., 437.

15. J. Gresham Machen, *What Is Faith?* (New York: Macmillan Publishing Company, Inc., 1925); *The Christian Faith in the Modern World* (New York: Macmillan Publishing Company, 1936); *The Christian View of Man* (Grand Rapids: Wm. B. Eerdmans Publishing Company, 1937).

16. Machen, *What Is Christianity?* 170.

17. Ibid., 102-03; Machen, *What Is Faith?* 47-48, 127-28, 151. Cf. *The New Testament: An Introduction to Its Literature and History* (Carlisle, PA: Banner of Truth, 1976) and also the discussions of this in Hart, "Princeton Mind"; Syd-

ney E. Ahlstrom, "The Scottish Philosophy and American Theology," *Church History* 24 (1955): 257ff.; George M. Marsden, "J. Gresham Machen, History, and Truth," *Westminster Theological Journal* 42 (1979-80): 157ff.

18. Machen, *Christian Faith in the Modern World*, 33ff.

19. Machen, *What Is Faith?* 23.

20. Ibid., 75ff.; Machen, *Christian Faith in the Modern World*, 117-18.

21. Machen, *What Is Christianity?* 24ff.

22. Stonehouse, *J. Gresham Machen*, 508.

23. Machen, *What Is Faith?* 171, 190ff., 207ff.; *The Christian Faith in the Modern World*, 152, 231ff.; *The Christian View of Man*, 164ff., 215-16, 289, 296.

24. Machen, *What Is Faith?* 59-60, 65-66; *The Christian View of Man*, 84ff.; *What Is Christianity?* 141, 304ff.

25. Ibid., 181, 190-91, 203, 209.

26. Ibid., 135ff., 190-91, 207-08; Machen, *Christian View of Man*, 175-76, 288, 291.

27. Cf. M. Karlberg, "Justification in Redemptive History," *Westminster Theological Journal* 43 (1981): 213-14.

28. Machen, *What Is Christianity?* 240.

29. Machen, *Christianity and Liberalism* (Philadelphia: Presbyterian Guardian, 1940), 136, 146-47.

30. Ibid., 147-48.

31. Machen, *Christian View of Man*, 84ff.

32. Machen, *What Is Faith?* 54.

33. Machen, "Christian Scholarship and the Defence of the Faith," in *What Is Christianity?* 126ff.; *Christianity and Liberalism*, Introduction.

34. Cf. his comments on McGiffert in *What Is Faith?* 54ff.; cf. also 210ff., 234ff., and Stonehouse, *J. Gresham Machen*, 473ff.

35. Cf. n. 23.

36. Cf. Machen, *What Is Christianity?* 126ff., 138ff.

37. Cf. Machen, "The Christian View of Missions," in *What Is Christianity?* 148ff.

38. Machen, *What is Faith?* 103; *Christian View of Man*, 131ff.

39. Machen, *What Is Christianity?* 224ff.; Stonehouse, *J. Gresham Machen*, chs. 22-23.

40. Ibid., chs. 40-41.

41. Machen, *What Is Christianity?* 271.

42. Ibid., 267ff.; Machen, *Christian View of Man*, 227ff.; *What Is Faith?* 181; *Christian View of Man*, 10.

43. Machen, "The Necessity of the Christian School," in *What Is Christianity?* 248ff.

44. Ibid., 296ff.; Machen, *What Is Faith?* 15ff.

45. Ibid., 15ff.

46. Ibid., 18ff., 103ff., 184.

47. Ibid., 15ff.

48. Ibid., 18ff., 103ff., 184.

BIBLIOGRAPHY

1. Bibliographies and Indexes

It should be noted that many of the works listed in Section 4 contain extensive bibliographical material on the Princetonians as well.

Armstrong, William P. "Index of *The Presbyterian and Reformed Review* XI (1900)–XIII (1902) and *The Princeton Theological Review* I (1903)–XXVII (1929)." *Princeton Theological Review* 27 (July 1929): 487–587.

Biblical Repertory and Princeton Review. Index Volume from 1825 to 1868. Philadelphia: Peter Walker, 1870–1871.

Burr, Nelson R. "The Princeton Theology." In *A Critical Bibliography of Religion in America*, vol. IV, parts 3, 4, and 5, pp. 999–1003 of *Religion in American Life*, edited by James Ward Smith and A. Leland Jamison. Princeton: Princeton University Press, 1961.

Dulles, Joseph H. "Index to Volumes I–X, 1890–1899." *Presbyterian and Reformed Review* 10 (October 1899): 727–98.

Gapp, Kenneth S. "The *Princeton Review* Series and the Contribution of Princeton Theological Seminary to Presbyterian Quarterly Magazines." Typescript, Speer Library, Princeton Theological Seminary, 1960.

Kennedy, Earl William. "Authors of Articles in the *Biblical Repertory and Princeton Review.*" Typescript, Speer Library, Princeton Theological Seminary, 1963.

_____. "Writings about Charles Hodge and His Works. Principally as Found in Periodicals Contained in the Speer Library of Princeton Theological Seminary for the Years 1830–1880." Typescript, Speer Library, Princeton Theological Seminary, 1963.

Meeter, John E., and Nicole, Roger. *A Bibliography of Benjamin Breckinridge Warfield 1851–1921.* Nutley, NJ: Presbyterian and Reformed, 1974.

2. Major Books of the Major Princeton Theologians

This partial list of published books also contains information on where these various volumes are still in print (as of 1981–1982 catalogs). For each author, books are listed in chronological order by date of first publication. Many of these works went through several editions in their authors' own lifetimes.

Archibald Alexander

A Brief Outline of the Evidence of the Christian Religion. Princeton: D.A. Borrenstein, 1825.

The Canon of the Old and New Testaments Ascertained; or, The Bible Complete Without the Apocrypha and Unwritten Traditions. New York: D.A. Borrenstein for G. & C. Carvill, 1826.

Evidences of the Authenticity, Inspiration, and Canonical Authority of the Holy Scriptures. Philadelphia: Presbyterian Board of Publication, 1826. In print, Arno and New York Times, New York.

A Selection of Hymns, Adapted to the Devotions of the Closet, the Family and the Social Circle. New York: Leavitt, 1831.

Counsels of the Aged to the Young. Philadelphia: Key and Biddle, 1833.

History of the Patriarchs. Philadelphia: American Sunday School Union, 1833.

History of the Israelites, from the Death of Joseph to the Death of Moses. Philadelphia: Perkins, 1834.

Thoughts on Religious Experience. Philadelphia: Presbyterian Board of Publication, 1841. In print, Banner of Truth, London.

Biographical Sketches of the Founder and Principal Alumni of the Log College. Princeton: J. T. Robenson, 1845. In print, Banner of Truth, London.

A Brief Compend of Bible Truth. Philadelphia: Presbyterian Board of Publication, 1846.

A History of Colonization on the Western Coast of Africa. Philadelphia: Martien, 1846. In print, Arno and New York Times, New York; Greenwood, Westport, CT.

Theological Essays. New York and London, 1846.

Practical Sermons: To Be Read in Families and Social Meetings. Philadelphia: Presbyterian Board of Publication, 1850.

Outlines of Moral Science. New York: Charles Scribner's Sons, 1852.

A History of the Israelitish Nation, from Their Origin to Their Dispersion at the Destruction of Jerusalem by the Romans. Philadelphia: Martien, 1853.

Practical Truths. New York: American Tract Society, 1857.

Charles Hodge

A Commentary on the Epistle to the Romans. Philadelphia: Grigg & Elliot, 1835. In print, Eerdmans, Grand Rapids; Banner of Truth, London.

The Constitutional History of the Presbyterian Church in the United States of America. Philadelphia: Presbyterian Board of Education, 1840.

The Way of Life. Philadelphia: American Sunday School Union, 1841. In print, Baker, Grand Rapids; Banner of Truth, London. New edition, edited by Mark A. Noll. Mahwah, NJ: Paulist, 1987.

A Commentary on the Epistle to the Ephesians. New York: Carter & Bros., 1856. In print, Baker, Grand Rapids.

Essays and Reviews: Selected from the Princeton Review. New York: Carter & Bros. 1857. In print, Garland, New York.

An Exposition of the First Epistle to the Corinthians. New York: Carter & Bros., 1857. In print, Eerdmans, Grand Rapids; Baker, Grand Rapids; Banner of Truth, London.

An Exposition of the Second Epistle to the Corinthians. New York: Carter & Bros., 1857. In print, Baker, Grand Rapids; Banner of Truth, London.

Systematic Theology. New York: Charles Scribner's Sons, 1872–1873. In print, Eerdmans, Grand Rapids; J. Clarke, Cambridge, England.

What Is Darwinism? New York: Scribners, Armstrong and Company, 1874.

Conference Papers. New York: Charles Scribner's Sons, 1879. In print, as *Princeton Sermons,* Banner of Truth, London.

A. A. Hodge

Outlines of Theology. New York: Carter & Bros., 1860. Rev. and enlarged ed., 1878. In print, Zondervan, Grand Rapids.

The Atonement. Philadelphia: Presbyterian Board of Publication, 1867.

A Commentary on the Confession of Faith. Philadelphia: Presbyterian Board of Publication, 1889. In print, Banner of Truth, London.

The Life of Charles Hodge. New York: Charles Scribner's Sons, 1880. In print, Arno and New York Times, New York.

Inspiration, with B.B. Warfield. Philadelphia: Presbyterian Board of Publication, 1881. In print, Baker, Grand Rapids, with notes, introduction, and bibliographies by Roger R. Nicole.

Popular Lectures on Theological Themes. Philadelphia: Presbyterian Board of Publication, 1887. In print as *Evangelical Theology,* Banner of Truth, London.

B. B. Warfield

An Introduction to the Textual Criticism of the New Testament. London: Hodder and Stoughton, 1886.

The Power of God Unto Salvation. Philadelphia: Presbyterian Board of Publication, 1903.

The Lord of Glory. New York: American Tract Society, 1907.

The Saviour of the World. New York: Hodder and Stoughton, 1914.

The Plan of Salvation. Philadelphia: Presbyterian Board of Publication, 1915. In print, Eerdmans, Grand Rapids.

Faith and Life. "Conferences" in the Oratory of Princeton Seminary. New York: Longmans, Green, 1916. In print, Banner of Truth, London.

Counterfeit Miracles. New York: Charles Scribner's Sons, 1918. In print, Banner of Truth, London.

Revelation and Inspiration, Works: Vol. I. New York: Oxford University Press, 1927. In print, Baker, Grand Rapids.

Biblical Doctrines, Works: Vol. II. New York: Oxford University Press, 1929. In print, Baker, Grand Rapids.

Christology and Criticism, Works: Vol. III. New York: Oxford University Press, 1931. In print, Baker, Grand Rapids.

Studies in Tertullian and Augustine, Works: Vol. IV. New York: Oxford University Press, 1930. In print, Baker, Grand Rapids; Greenwood, Westport, CT.

Calvin and Calvinism, Works: Vol. V. New York: Oxford University Press, 1931. In print, Baker, Grand Rapids.

The Westminster Assembly and Its Work, Works: Vol. VI. New York: Oxford University Press, 1931. In print, Baker, Grand Rapids.

Perfectionism Part One, Works: Vol. VII. New York: Oxford University Press, 1931. In print, Baker, Grand Rapids.

Perfectionism Part Two, Works: Vol. VIII. New York: Oxford University Press, 1931. In print, Baker, Grand Rapids.

Studies in Theology, Works: Vol. IX. New York: Oxford University Press, 1932. In print, Baker, Grand Rapids.

Critical Reviews, Works: Vol. X. New York: Oxford University Press, 1932. In print, Baker, Grand Rapids.

The Inspiration and Authority of the Bible [selected mostly from *Works, Vol. I*]. Philadelphia: Presbyterian and Reformed, 1948.

The Person and Work of Christ [selected mostly from *Works, Vol. III*]. Philadelphia: Presbyterian and Reformed, 1950.

Biblical and Theological Studies [selected mostly from *Works, Vol. II*]. Philadelphia: Presbyterian and Reformed, 1952.

Calvin and Augustine [selected from *Works, Vols. IV* and *V*]. Philadelphia: Presbyterian and Reformed, 1956.

Perfectionism [selected from *Works, Vols. VII* and *VIII*]. Philadelphia: Presbyterian and Reformed, 1958.

Selected Shorter Writings of Benjamin B. Warfield, Vols. I and *II*. Edited by John E. Meeter. Nutley, NJ: Presbyterian and Reformed, 1970 and 1973.

3. Secondary Works

Princeton Seminary and General Studies on the Princeton Theology

Balmer, Randall H. "The Princetonians and Scripture: A Reconsideration." *Westminster Theological Journal* 44 (1982): 352–65.

_____. "The Princetonians, Scripture, and Recent Scholarship." *Journal of Presbyterian History* 60 (Fall 1982): 267–70.

Biographical Catalogue of the Princeton Theological Seminary, 1815–1932, compiled by Edward Howell Roberts. Princeton: Trustees of the Theological Seminary of the Presbyterian Church, 1933.

The Centennial Celebration of the Theological Seminary of the Presbyterian Church in the United States of America at Princeton, New Jersey. Princeton: Princeton Theological Seminary, 1912.

Hart, John W. "Princeton Theological Seminary: The Reorganization of 1929." *Journal of Presbyterian History* 58 (Summer 1980): 124–40.

Hodge, Charles. "Retrospect of the History of the Princeton Review." *Biblical Repertory and Princeton Review. Index Volume*, no. 1 (January 1870): 1–39.

Hoffecker, W. Andrew. "The Devotional Life of Archibald Alexander, Charles Hodge, and Benjamin B. Warfield." *Westminster Theological Journal* 42 (Fall 1979): 111–29.

_____. *Piety and the Princeton Theologians: Archibald Alexander, Charles Hodge, and Benjamin Warfield.* Phillipsburg, NJ: Presbyterian and Reformed; and Grand Rapids: Baker, 1981.

Illick, Joseph E., III. "The Reception of Darwinism at the Theological Seminary and the College at Princeton, New Jersey." *Journal of the Presbyterian Historical Society* 38 (September 1960): 152–65; (December 1960): 234–43.

Linsay, Thomas M. "The Doctrine of Scripture: The Reformers and the Princeton School," In *The Expositor*, Fifth Series, edited by W. Robertson Nicoll, 1:278–93. London: Hodder and Stoughton, 1895.

Noll, Mark A. "The Founding of Princeton Seminary." *Westminster Theological Journal* 42 (Fall 1979): 72–110.

Sandeen, Ernest R. "The Princeton Theology: One Source of Biblical Literalism in American Protestantism." *Church History* 31 (September 1962): 307–21.

Vander Stelt, John C. *Philosophy and Scripture: A Study in Old Princeton and Westminster Theology.* Marlton, NJ.: Mack, 1978.

Woodbridge, John D., and Balmer, Randy. "The Princetonians' Viewpoint of Biblical Authority: An Evaluation of Ernest Sandeen." In *Scripture and Truth*, edited by John D. Woodbridge and D.A. Carson. Grand Rapids: Zondervan, 1983.

Archibald Alexander

Alexander, James Waddel. *The Life of Archibald Alexander.* New York: Charles Scribner's Sons, 1854.

"Archibald Alexander." *Biblical Repertory and Princeton Review. Index Volume*, no. 1 (January 1870): 42–67.

De Witt, John. "Archibald Alexander's Preparation for His Professorship." *Princeton Theological Review* 3 (October 1905): 573–94.

Hodge, Charles. "Memoir of Archibald Alexander." *Biblical Repertory and Princeton Review* 27 (January 1855): 133–59.

Jackson, Gordon E. "Archibald Alexander's *Thoughts on Religious Experience*, a Critical Revisiting." *Journal of Presbyterian History* 51 (Summer 1973): 141–54.

Loetscher, Lefferts A. *Facing the Enlightenment and Pietism: Archibald Alexander and the Founding of Princeton Theological Seminary* (Westport, CT: Greenwood, 1983).

Mackay, John A. "Archibald Alexander (1772–1851): Founding Father." In *Sons of the Prophets*, edited by Hugh T. Kerr. Princeton: Princeton University Press, 1963.

McKim, Donald K. "Archibald Alexander and the Doctrine of Scripture." *Journal of Presbyterian History* 54 (Fall 1976): 355–75.

Nelson, John Oliver. "Archibald Alexander, Winsome Conservative." *Journal of the Presbyterian Historical Society* 35 (March 1957): 15–33.

Okholm, Dennis. "Biblical Inspiration and Infallibility in the Writings of Archibald Alexander." *Trinity Journal* [Trinty Evangelical Divinity School] 5 (Spring 1976): 79–89.

Charles Hodge

Barker, William S. "The Social Views of Charles Hodge (1797–1878): A Study in Nineteenth-Century Calvinism and Conservatism." *Presbyterion: Covenant Seminary Review* 1 (Spring 1975): 1–22.

Cashdollar, Charles D. "The Pursuit of Piety: Charles Hodge's Diary, 1819–1820." *Journal of Presbyterian History* 55 (Fall 1977): 267–74.

"Charles Hodge." *Biblical Repertory and Princeton Review. Index Volume*, no. 2 (1870): 200–11.

Danhof, Ralph J. *Charles Hodge as Dogmatician*. Goes, The Netherlands: Oosterbaan and le Cointre, 1929.

Discourses Commemorative of the Life and Work of Charles Hodge. Philadelphia: Henry B. Ashmead, 1879.

Hodge, Archibald Alexander. *The Life of Charles Hodge*. New York: Charles Scribner's Sons, 1880.

Hogeland, Ronald W. "Charles Hodge, The Association of Gentlemen and Ornamental Womanhood: A Study of Male Conventional Wisdom, 1825–1855." *Journal of Presbyterian History* 53 (Fall 1975): 239–55.

Holifield, E. Brooks. "Mercersburg, Princeton, and the South: The Sacramental Controversy in the Nineteenth Century." *Journal of Presbyterian History* 54 (Summer 1976): 238–57.

Nelson, John Oliver. "Charles Hodge (1797–1878): Nestor of Orthodoxy." In *The Lives of Eighteen from Princeton*, edited by Willard Thorp. Princeton: Princeton University Press, 1946.

Olbricht, Thomas H. "Charles Hodge as an American New Testament Interpreter." *Journal of Presbyterian History* 57 (Summer 1979): 117–33.

Patton, Francis Landey. "Charles Hodge." *Presbyterian Review* 2 (January 1881): 349–77.

Proceedings Connected with the Semi-Centennial Commemorative of the Professorship of Rev. Charles Hodge, D.D., LL.D., April 24, 1872. New York: Anson D.F. Randolph, 1872.

Shriver, George H. "Passages in Friendship: John W. Nevin to Charles Hodge, 1872." *Journal of Presbyterian History* 58 (Summer 1980): 116–22.

Stein, Stephen J. "Stuart and Hodge on Romans 5:12–21: An Exegetical Controversy about Original Sin." *Journal of Presbyterian History* 47 (December 1969): 340–58.

Wells, David F. "The Stout and Persistent 'Theology' of Charles Hodge." *Christianity Today,* August 30, 1974, pp. 10–15.

A. A. Hodge

Patton, Francis Landey. *A Discourse in Memory of Archibald Alexander Hodge.* Philadelphia: Times, 1887.

Paxton, William M. *Address Delivered at the Funeral of Archibald Alexander Hodge.* New York: Anson D. F. Randolph, 1886.

Salmond, C. A. *Princetonian. Charles & A. A. Hodge: With Class and Table Talk of Hodge the Younger.* Edinburgh: Oliphant, Anderson & Ferrier, 1888.

B. B. Warfield

Allis, O.T. "Personal Impressions of Dr. Warfield." *Banner of Truth* 89 (Fall 1971): 10–14.

Craig, Samuel G. "Benjamin B. Warfield." In *Biblical and Theological Studies,* pp. xi–xlviii. Philadelphia: Presbyterian and Reformed, 1952.

Fuller, Daniel P. "Benjamin B. Warfield"s View of Faith and History." *Journal of the Evangelical Theological Society* 11 (Spring 1968): 75–83.

Gerstner, John H. "Warfield's Case for Biblical Inerrancy." In *God's Inerrant Word,* edited by John Warwick Montgomery. Minneapolis: Bethany, 1974.

Grier, W.J. "Benjamin Breckinridge Warfield." *Banner of Truth* 89 (Fall 1971): 3–9.

Krabbendam, Hendrick. "B. B. Warfield vs. G.C. Berkouwer on Scripture." In *Inerrancy: The Extent of Biblical Authority,* edited by Norman L. Geisler. Grand Rapids: Zondervan, 1980.

Murray, Iain et al., eds. "Warfield Commemorative Issue, 1921–1971." *Banner of Truth* 89 (Fall 1971).

Nicole, Roger. "The Inspiration of Scripture: B.B. Warfield and Dr. Dewey M. Beegle." *Gordon Review* 8 (Winter 1964–65): 93–109.

Parsons, Mike. "Warfield and Scripture." *The Churchman* (London) 91 (July 1977): 198–220.

Patton, Francis L. "Benjamin Breckinridge Warfield—A Memorial Address." *Princeton Theological Review* 19 (July 1921): 369–91.

Peter, J.F. "Warfield on the Scriptures." *Reformed Theological Review* 16 (October 19, 1957): 76–84.

Rogers, Jack B. "Van Til and Warfield on Scripture in the Westminister Confession." In *Jerusalem and Athens,* edited by E.R. Geehan. Nutley, NJ: Presbyterian and Reformed, 1971.

Swanton, Robert. "Warfield and Progressive Orthodoxy." *Reformed Theological Review* 23 (October 1964): 74–87.

Torrance, T.F. Review of Warfield's *Inspiration and Authority of the Bible. Scottish Journal of Theology* 7 (March 1854): 104–8.

Wallis, Wilbut B. "Benjamin B. Warfield: Didactic and Polemical Theologian." *Presbyterion: Covenant Seminary Review* 3 (April 1977): 73–94.

Westblade, Donald. "Benjamin B. Warfield on Inspiration and Inerrancy." *Studia Biblica et Theologica* 10 (April 1980): 27–43.

4. Theological, Intellectual, Cultural, Denominational Background

The following are works which place the Princeton theologians in their historical and theological contexts. Many of them contain extensive material on the Princeton theology and the relationship of that theology to wider spheres of Christian and American life.

Ahlstrom, Sydney E. *A Religious History of the American People.* New Haven: Yale University Press, 1972.

_____. "Theology in America: A Historical Survey." In *The Shaping of American Religion,* edited by James Ward Smith and A. Leland Jamison. Princeton: Princeton University Press, 1961.

_____. *Theology in America: The Major Protestant Voices from Puritanism to Neo-Orthodoxy.* Indianapolis: Bobbs-Merrill, 1967.

_____. "The Scottish Philosophy and American Theology." *Church History* 24 (1955): 257–72.

Armstrong, Maurice W. et al., eds. *The Presbyterian Experience: Sources of American Presbyterian History.* Philadelphia: Westminster, 1956.

Baird, Robert. *Religion in the United States of America.* Reprint. New York: Arno and New York Times, 1969 [1844].

Barker, William S. "Inerrancy and the Role of the Bible's Authority: A Review Article." *Presbyterion: Covenant Seminary Review* 6 (Fall 1980): 96–107.

Beardslee, John W., III, ed. and trans. *Reformed Dogmatics: Seventeenth-Century Theology Through the Writings of Wollebius, Voetius, and Turretin.* New York: Oxford University Press, 1965. Reprint. Grand Rapids: Baker, 1977.

Berkhof, Louis. *Introduction to Systematic Theology.* Grand Rapids: Eerdmans, 1932. Reprint. Grand Rapids: Baker, 1979.

Bowden, Henry Warner. *Church History in the Age of Science: Historiographical Patterns in the United States 1876–1918.* Chapel Hill: University of North Carolina Press, 1971.

Bozeman, Theodore Dwight. *Protestants in an Age of Science: The Baconian Ideal and Antebellum American Religious Thought.* Chapel Hill: University of North Carolina Press, 1977.

Brown, Ira V. "The Higher Criticism Comes to America, 1880–1900." *Journal of the Presbyterian Historical Society* 38 (December 1960): 193–212.

Brown, Jerry Wayne. *The Rise of Biblical Criticism in America, 1800–1870: The New England Scholars.* Middletown, CT: Wesleyan University Press, 1969.

Cecil, Anthony C. *The Theological Development of Edwards Amasa Park, Last of the Consistent Calvinists.* Missoula, MT: Scholars Press, 1974.

Collins, Varnum Lansing. *President Witherspoon*. New York: Arno and New York Times, 1968 [1925].

Conforti, Joseph A. *Samuel Hopkins and the New Divinity Movement*. Washington and Grand Rapids: Eerdmans (for the Christian University Press), 1981.

Cross, Barbara M. *Horace Bushnell: Minister to a Changing America*. Chicago: University of Chicago Press, 1958.

Dillenberger, John. *Protestant Thought and Natural Science: A Historical Study*. Nashville: Abingdon, 1960.

Dollar, George W. *A History of Fundamentalism in America*. Greenville, SC: Bob Jones University Press, 1973.

Finney, Charles G. *Memoirs of Rev. Charles G. Finney, Written by Himself*. Reprint. New York: AMS Press, 1973 [1876].

Foster, Frank H. *A Genetic History of the New England Theology*. Chicago: University of Chicago Press, 1907.

Geehan, E.R., ed. *Jerusalem and Athens: Critical Discussions on the Philosophy and Apologetics of Cornelius Van Til*. Nutley, NJ: Presbyterian and Reformed, 1971.

General Catalogue of Princeton University 1746–1906.Princeton: Princeton University Press, 1908.

Grave, S.A. *The Scottish Philosophy of Common Sense*. Oxford: Clarendon Press, 1960.

Haroutunian, Joseph. *Piety Versus Moralism: The Passing of the New England Theology*. New York: Holt, 1932.

Hatch, Nathan O., and Noll, Mark A., eds. *The Bible in America: Essays in Cultural History*. New York: Oxford University Press, 1982.

Hoeveler, J. David, Jr. *James McCosh and the Scottish Intellectual Tradition*. Princeton: Princeton University Press, 1981.

Hofstadter, Richard. "The Revolution in Higher Education." In *Paths of American Thought*, edited by A.M. Schlesinger, Jr., and Morton White. Boston: Houghton Mifflin, 1963.

Holifield, E. Brooks. *The Gentlemen Theologians: American Theology in Southern Culture, 1795–1860*. Durham, NC: Duke University Press, 1978.

Hood, Fred J. *Reformed America: The Middle and Southern States, 1783–1837*. University, AL: University of Alabama Press, 1980.

Hovenkamp, Herbert. *Science and Religion in America, 1800–1860*. Philadelphia: University of Pennsylvania Press, 1978.

Howe, Daniel Walker. *The Unitarian Conscience: Harvard Moral Philosophy, 1805–1861*. Cambridge: Harvard University Press, 1970.

_____, ed. *Victorian America*. Philadelphia: University of Pennsylvania Press, 1976.

Hudson, Winthrop S. *Religion in America*. 3d ed., New York: Charles Scribner's Sons, 1981.

Hutchison, George P. *The History Behind the Reformed Presbyterian Church, Evangelical Synod*. Cherry Hill, NJ: Mack, 1974.

_____. *The Problem of Original Sin in American Presbyterian Theology*. Nutley, NJ: Presbyterian and Reformed, 1972.

Hutchison, William R. *The Modernist Impulse in American Protestantism.* Cambridge: Harvard University Press, 1976.

Kelsey, David H. *The Uses of Scripture in Recent Theology.* Philadelphia: Fortress, 1975.

Kuyper, Abraham. *Principles of Sacred Theology.* Translated by J. Hendrik De Vries. Introduction by B.B. Warfield. Reprint. Grand Rapids: Baker, 1980 [1898].

Loetscher, Lefferts. *The Broadening Church: A Study of Theological Issues in the Presbyterian Church Since 1869.* Philadelphia: University of Pennsylvania Press, 1957.

McLachlan, James, and Harrison, Richard A., eds. *Princetonians: A Biographical Dictionary.* Princeton: Princeton University Press, 1976.

Marsden, George M. "The Collapse of American Evangelical Academia." In *Faith and Rationality,* edited by Nicholas Wolterstorff. Notre Dame, IN: University of Notre Dame Press, 1983.

_____. *The Evangelical Mind and the New School Presbyterian Experience.* New Haven: Yale University Press, 1970.

_____. *Fundamentalism and American Culture: The Shaping of Twentieth-Century American Evangelicalism.* New York: Oxford University Press, 1980.

_____. "On Being Reformed: Our Present Tasks in the American Setting." *Reformed Journal* (September 1981): 14–17.

May, Henry F. *The Enlightenment in America.* New York: Oxford University Press, 1976.

Meyer, D.H. *The Instructed Conscience: The Shaping of the American National Ethic.* Philadelphia: University of Pennsylvania Press, 1972.

Miller, Perry. *The Life of the Mind in America from the Revolution to the Civil War.* New York: Harcourt, Brace and World, 1965.

Moore, James R. *The Post-Darwinian Controversies: A Study of the Protestant Struggle to Come to Terms with Darwin in Great Britain and America, 1870–1900.* Cambridge: Cambridge University Press, 1979.

Nichols, James Hastings, ed. *The Mercersburg Theology.* New York: Oxford University Press 1966.

_____. *Romanticism in American Theology: Nevin and Schaff at Mercersburg.* Chicago: University of Chicago Press, 1961.

Noll, Mark A. "Christian Thinking and the Rise of the American University." *Christian Scholar's Review* 9 (1979): 3–16.

_____. "Who Sets the Stage for Understanding Scripture? Philosophies of Science Often Provide the Logic for Our Hermeneutics." *Christianity Today,* May 23, 1980, pp. 14–18.

Numbers, Ronald L. *Creation by Natural Law: Laplace's Nebular Hypothesis in American Thought.* Seattle: University of Washington Press, 1977.

Oleson, Alexandra, and Brown, Sanborn C., eds. *The Pursuit of Knowledge in the Early American Republic: American Scientific and Learned Societies from Colonial Times to the Civil War.* Baltimore: Johns Hopkins University Press, 1976.

Oleson, Alexandra, and Voss, John, eds. *The Organization of Knowledge in Modern America, 1860–1920.* Baltimore: Johns Hopkins University Press, 1979.

Rennie, Ian. "Mixed Metaphors, Misunderstood Models, and Puzzling Paradigms: A Contemporary Effort to Correct Some Current Misunderstandings Regarding the Authority and Interpretation of the Bible. An Historical Response." Typescript, Institute for Christian Studies, Toronto, 1981.

Reynolds, David S. *Faith in Fiction: The Emergence of Religious Literature in America.* Cambridge: Harvard University Press, 1981.

Rogers, Jack Bartlett. *Scripture in the Westminster Confession: A Problem of Historical Interpretation for American Presbyterianism.* Grand Rapids: Eerdmans, 1967.

Rogers, Jack Bartlett, and McKim, Donald K. *The Authority and Interpretation of the Bible: An Historical Approach.* San Francisco: Harper & Row, 1979.

Sandeen, Ernest R. *The Roots of Fundamentalism: British and American Millenarianism 1800–1930.* Chicago: University of Chicago Press, 1970.

Saum, Lewis O. *The Popular Mood of Pre-Civil War America.* Westport, CT: Greenwood, 1980.

Sloan, Douglas. *The Scottish Enlightenment and the American College Ideal.* New York: Teacher's College Press, 1961.

Smith, Elwyn. *The Presbyterian Minstry in American Culture.* Philadelphia: Westminster, 1962.

Smith, Gary S. "The Spirit of Capitalism Revisited: Calvinists in the Industrial Revolution." *Journal of Presbyterian History* 59 (Winter 1981): 481–97.

Smith, Hilrie Shelton. *Changing Conceptions of Original Sin: A Study in American Theology Since 1750.* New York: Charles Scribner's Sons, 1953.

———, ed. *Horace Bushnell.* New York: Oxford University Press, 1965.

Smith, Timothy L. *Revivalism and Social Reform in Mid-Nineteenth-Century America.* Nashville: Abingdon, 1957.

Turretin, Francis. *The Doctrine of Scripture.* Edited and translated by John W. Beardslee III. Grand Rapids: Baker, 1981.

Van Til, Cornelius. *The Defense of the Faith.* 2d ed. Philadelphia: Presbyterian and Reformed, 1955.

Veysey, Laurence R. *The Emergence of the American University.* Chicago: University of Chicago Press, 1965.

Wells, David F. "Aftermath and Hindsight of the Atonement Debate." *Bibliotheca Sacra* 145 (1988): 3–14.

———. "American Society as Seen from the Nineteenth-Century Pulpit." *Bibliotheca Sacra* 144 (1987): 123–43.

———. "The Collision of Views on the Atonement." *Bibliotheca Sacra* 144 (1987): 363–76.

———. "Nathaniel William Taylor: Theologian of Revival." Typescript, July 1978.

———. "The Shaping of the Nineteenth-Century Debate over the Atonement." *Bibliotheca Sacra* 144 (1987): 243–53.

Welter, Rush. *The Mind of America 1820–1860.* New York: Columbia University Press, 1975.

Wertenbaker, Thomas Jefferson. *Princeton 1746–1896.* Princeton: Princeton University Press, 1946.

Willis, E. David. "The Material Assumptions of Integrative Theology: The Conditions of Experiential Church Dogmatics." *Princeton Seminary Bulletin,* n.s. 2 (1979): 232–50.

Woodbridge, John D. "Biblical Authority: Towards an Evaluation of the Rogers and McKim Proposal." *Trinity Journal,* n.s. 1 (Fall 1980): 165–236; expanded as *Biblical Authority: A Critique of the Rogers/McKim Proposal* (Grand Rapids: Zondervan, 1982).

Wright, Conrad. *The Beginnings of Unitarianism in America.* Boston: Starr King, 1955.

INDEX

DATE DUE
